The Self-Care Plan for Empaths

the
self-care
plan for
empaths

365 Days of Practices to Relax, Reduce Stress, and Manage Emotions

Katie Krimer, MA, LCSW

ROCKRIDGE PRESS

THIS BOOK BELONGS TO

_____

Contents

Introduction

Welcome to this little corner of solace and retreat, filled with a year's worth of daily support curated especially for the practice of taking care of *you*. It may seem uncomfortable or even daunting, as many of us empaths regularly miss out on intentional *me time*. However, it's important that we acknowledge the immense toll that the roles we naturally inhabit—as healers, nurturers, advocates, deep listeners, caretakers, mediators, feeling absorbers, perpetual givers, or peacemakers—take on our emotional, physical, and spiritual selves. By the time we've gone well past our limit, many empaths end up suffering from anxiety, self-neglect, moodiness, empathy fatigue, depression, burnout, and overwhelm. When we chronically mirror and absorb emotional and physical energy, the line between our feelings and others' can become blurry or nonexistent. Empaths are effortlessly open, which can leave them vulnerable to those who knowingly or unknowingly consume emotional energy. Even being in a room full of people that we don't know can be exhausting due to our high sensitivity to people's vibes. What's more, we get regularly bombarded by tragic news and scroll through social media feeds full of moving stories. Even though we are *capable* of absorbing an uninterrupted stream of human energy—and maybe even thrive on it—it's crucial that we pay attention to its impact on our own mental well-being.

Of course, it's not all unpleasant! Let's also spend a few moments celebrating an empath's strengths and unique talents. Whether it is our deeply caring and understanding nature, our willingness to listen and make someone feel heard, or our unparalleled ability to offer supportive advice, we are often entrusted with the important task of holding nonjudgmental space for anyone struggling. Imagine being an empathetic ear for those who didn't have one available to them as children—it can be deeply rewarding. As empaths, our highly attuned nature gives us an uncanny ability to pick up on the most subtle of cues in behavior and tone. This attunement tends to go hand in hand with a superpower of intuition; our gut reactions very often prove accurate, even when we can't put a finger on what's giving us the "feeling" that something is off in a given situation. We can use these insights to inform our own decisions, as well as offer meaningful perspective to others. Did you know that aside from emotional empathy, there are empaths who feel super connected to the suffering of animals and the planet? For example, whenever I've driven past factories emitting smoke into the air, my throat tightens and I get queasy, as if I were, in fact, the earth, choking on toxins. Thankfully, my environmental empathy has moved me to make sustainability-forward changes in my life.

I'm hopeful that this book will bring you the little bit of daily care and healthy advice you need in order to restore your energy and to protect your special feeling powers from being regularly depleted. As a therapist for nearly ten years, I've had to learn how to be an emotional support for upward of forty people a week without taking their suffering home or burning out. Add to that my interactions with strangers who gravitate toward me to share their life stories, the conversations I have with every fellow dog walker and shop owner, and the energy required to be present in all of my meaningful personal relationships. I'm a proud, highly sensitive empath who has learned to harness my highly attuned mirror neurons for good without being overcome by a constant state of feeling all the feels. As you move through this self-care plan, know that you are in knowledgeable, warm, empathetic hands. It is possible to live in a mind space of safety and good mental and emotional health. I'm happy to show you how this is possible.

How to Use This Book

Soaking up every vibe around us means we need to find ways to regularly lighten our load. I'm betting that you've heard the word "self-care" thrown around plenty; it's a buzzword that pops up all over social media, doctors' offices, wellness centers, and is, of course, a favorite term among therapists. Perhaps you've heard suggestions to drink plenty of water, exercise, and meditate. Those are great suggestions for physical self-care, but they don't quite address the nuances of an empath's lived experience.

In the following pages, you'll find creative ways to engage with your spirit, your stresses, your environment, and your body. This 365-day-long journey will use four different methods to assist you in tuning into, honoring, and celebrating your (sensitive) inner being:

Journal prompts

Meditation exercises

Affirmations

Activities

Journal prompts will ask you to use your journal to dive deep into yourself to discover your optimal self-care rituals and path forward as a highly attuned individual. Brief meditation exercises will help you train your awareness and attention, and help you achieve a mentally clear and emotionally calm state throughout your journey. Affirmations, or mantras, will encourage you to speak positive statements to challenge and overcome self-sabotaging and negative thoughts. Activities will engage you to discover more about your empathic nature, as well as what you need from your relationships, environment, and body to live a life that serves you first, and others second. Each daily entry will tackle one method. Together, these methods will help you adopt a firm mindset of what self-care looks like for you, to practice the behaviors that will consistently bring your life the balance that it needs.

I recommend keeping this book on your bedside table and bookmarking each page as the year progresses. Either before going to sleep or upon waking up, flip to the current date's page and read the next couple of daily entries. Set the intention to engage with self-care and encourage yourself by remembering that a little bit can go a long way for your empathic soul. With practice and repetition, you will see how empowering it is to hold regular space for yourself without losing any of your gifts of holding space for others. You deserve to create intentional moments of reflection and rest.

JANUARY 1

My Empath Identity

The ability to observe and absorb others' emotions often affects an empath's identity, as the energy in that action is so consuming. You are encouraged to remember there are *many* aspects of who you are. In your journal, answer the following: How would your closest friends and loved ones describe you? What other qualities would you like them to notice, too?

JANUARY 2

Rise and Shine Meditation

The night before this meditation, set the intention that your morning session will fill you with the energy that you'll need to go throughout your day. When you awake, take three deep breaths, and softly gaze at the ceiling. As you continue to breathe, visualize a color that you associate with the absorption of stressful energy and a color that represents being in a state of peace and calm. For five to ten minutes, breathe in the color of calm and breathe out the color of anything you absorb, hold on to, or carry from your interactions with others. Imagine that when you're leaving bed to get ready for the day, your body is filled up with the color you associate with a peaceful state of being. Keep that color around you, and in your mind, as you move through your daily routine.

JANUARY 3

Own Your Energy

Practice owning the following statement:

I decide who receives my time and energy.
I choose how much energy I want to give away
in any moment. I protect and manage my energy.

JANUARY 4

Make a Self-Care Jar

As you embark on your path to becoming a self-caring empath, do your best to make the process fun and encouraging. Grab an empty jar and decorate it with paint, stickers, or other fun items so that it has some character. On pieces of paper, write down all the self-care practices you can think of, including those you may have already tried and loved, or new ones that scare you a little bit. Put them into the jar. When you catch yourself feeling drained or burnt out, grab one out of the jar and commit to practicing whatever is on that strip of paper. No double dips!

JANUARY 5

Pick the Right Battles

Not only are empaths highly attuned listeners, but they're also commonly the designated group therapist. This makes it difficult to separate from that 24/7 caretaking role to live in their own identity. In your journal, write about an experience where your highly attuned nature challenged you to resist involving yourself in another's personal struggle.

JANUARY 6

Breathing Peace Meditation

Moving through your days with a greater sense of underlying tranquility will help you feel more balanced, given the constant cycle of energy exchange you experience. Regular meditation practices will help strengthen your inner-peace muscles. At the beginning of your practice, find a comfortable seat and sit up with your back straight, but not tense. Close your eyes and begin to bring your awareness inward, letting any external stimuli pass on by. Take a deep breath in through your nose for four counts, and out through your mouth slowly for eight. Imagine that your breath is actually a vessel of peaceful energy. With each inhale, visualize the peacefulness being absorbed through your nostrils and other pores in your body. As you breathe out, say goodbye to any chaos or stress. Repeat the following: "I breathe in peace" and "I breathe out stress."

JANUARY 7

Soothe Worries

When you feel worried or anxious, say:

There is infinite space to hold even the most unpleasant of emotions. The more space I create, the smaller the struggle becomes.

JANUARY 8

Shift from Empathy to Compassion

As an empath, constantly sharing or taking on others' feelings is the ultimate breeding ground for burnout. This visualization activity will help shift you into a state of compassion. There, you can acknowledge others' pain from a place of awareness without co-experiencing feelings.

Close your eyes and visualize a situation in which you acutely felt someone else's pain. Picture yourself offering comfort without having a personal emotional response. Inhale to breathe in your desire to support; exhale to breathe out any emotions that aren't yours. This is a great tool to use when you need to think fast and move through oncoming energies.

JANUARY 9

Build Self-Awareness

Becoming more aware of your emotional state will make it easier to know what your feelings are in any given moment. In your journal, make a list of five difficult emotions you regularly experience. Select one from the list to focus on. What do you typically do to address this particular feeling in your body?

JANUARY 10

That's a Wrap! Meditation

This meditation is a great self-care technique to use at the end of a taxing day. Keep it in your empath tool kit to use at the end of any future stressful days.

As you settle into bed for the night, lie in a comfortable position with your legs apart. Gently lay your arms at your sides. Close your eyes and take a few deep breaths to settle in. As you breathe in through your nose, feel your body begin to sink into the mattress. As you breathe out through your mouth, let it sink farther. Pay attention to the curve of your spine as you visualize the relaxation of any contracting muscles. Continue these deep breaths and notice the sensation of the mattress cradling your body. Imagine releasing all the emotions from the day at the end of each exhale. Let it all go.

JANUARY 11

This Is Not My Pain

When you know you've taken on someone else's suffering, say:

This is not my pain. I am not in control of someone else's experience. I release it with compassion.

JANUARY 12

What Drains My Energy?

As you work through your self-care plan, be sure to monitor your energy reserves. Journal about what currently drains your energy. Ask yourself, "What boundaries can I establish to protect my inner self?"

JANUARY 13

Use Breath to Find Presence

Empaths often struggle with remaining present because they are consumed or distracted by anything outside of themselves with an emotional pull. Becoming aware of your breath is a way to ground yourself in the present moment. Sit or lie down in a comfortable position. Start by inhaling through your nose and begin to pay attention to the flow of air as it enters the nostrils. Follow the breath as it enters your windpipe and moves onto the lungs and belly. On the out-breath, notice the sound of air as your lips purse to push it out. When your mind wanders, come back to the breath.

JANUARY 14

Release Tension Meditation

When you absorb and observe negative energy, it creates toxicity in your body, mind, and heart. This can lead to illness. Loving self-care means learning how to expel this tension.

Sit or lie in a comfortable position and begin to take deep breaths, inhaling through the nose and exhaling through the mouth. Bring your attention to a part of your body where you notice tension or tightness, like your shoulders or chest. Visualize that part of your body in your mind as if you were looking at it in real life. With each in-breath, vividly picture the muscles knotted and tight. With each out-breath, consciously direct that part of your body to relax and release. With every set of breaths, relax other parts of your body where stress has settled in.

JANUARY 15

Give Up Control

Remind yourself:

I can witness another's struggle without participating in it. I excuse myself from the need to manage others' thoughts, emotions, or choices.

JANUARY 16

What Was Viewed as Weakness

Empaths are often viewed as being too emotional or overly sensitive. Recall a time when your empathic nature was questioned as something negative. Write down one way you could respond now, as a confident and aware empath.

JANUARY 17

Separate from Emotions

The spongelike nature of empaths put them at risk for overidentifying with the feelings that others are experiencing. Without a conscious boundary, you can lose sight of which emotions are *yours* and become caught up in their intensity. Take five photos of yourself. Use a different facial expression in each photo to demonstrate a challenging emotion. Print them out. On the back of each photo, label the emotion and write a consequence of feeling it too intensely. Then write one way you can address the emotion in a healthier way when it arises. Keep these photos as reminders for your boundary practice when you are holding on to a difficult emotion.

JANUARY 18

Music in My Ears Meditation

Pick a genre of instrumental music—classical, jazz, blues, etc.—and play it at a volume where you can hear it but it does not overwhelm the senses. Let your eyes close, and set the intention to rest your awareness on the sounds and instruments that you hear. When a thought comes or you notice your mind wandering, bring your mind's focus to the music. You can even gently say "music" to yourself, so that you can turn your attention back to listening. Allow your mind to find its focus on various melodies throughout the song. Follow the sound of a particular instrument. When your mind wanders, bring your attention back to the instrument you've chosen.

JANUARY 19

Being among Many

Before heading into a space with a group of people, affirm to yourself:

I put up a protective mental shield that prevents excess energy from coming in or out.

JANUARY 20

What Are My Boundaries?

In relationships, a boundary is a limit, or space, between you and another person. It's where the other person stops and you begin. Boundaries help protect your inner peace and stability, a crucial part of self-care. Answer the following: In what relationships could I establish better boundaries? What would they look like? What purpose will they serve for me?

JANUARY 21

Practice a Nighttime Ritual

Getting a good night's sleep is imperative to lowering stress levels and allowing your busy mind to rest without any cognitive or emotional demands. This bedtime routine will help increase your chances of a deeper, more restful sleep. Get into your favorite pajamas, brush your teeth, and take care of your skin. Back in your bedroom, stretch for five minutes to release any tightness, meditate for five to ten minutes, slip under the covers mindfully, and say aloud three things you're grateful for from the day. If you already have a routine, choose at least one more new step that you would enjoy incorporating.

JANUARY 22

Picture Peace Meditation

There is benefit in retreating to a safe place away from what is making you tired. For this meditation, imagine the details of a place—real or fantasy—where the only thing required of you is to rest. Perhaps you're walking atop a windy mountain or lying on the beach and hearing the sounds of the waves crashing against the shore. As you breathe in deeply and breathe out completely, take your mind to that tranquil space. A soft smile might naturally form—let it invite you further into this imagined place where there is nothing but tranquility and stillness. If you don't have the time to meditate, call to mind the place that you've chosen anytime you need tranquility.

JANUARY 23

Take Time Out

Saving time for intentional and loving self-care isn't always easy. Work demands, responsibilities at home, and relationships all require a lot of attention. Ultimate self-care practices for empaths means scheduling time in daily schedules to recharge. What self-care breaks do you take during the day? What would you like to try?

JANUARY 24

Recognizing Feel-Good Emotions

Although you're able to experience the feelings of others, you are not exclusively tied to the difficult ones. As an empath, you also experience joy, love, and excitement at your very core. Don't forget to tune in to feelings that fill you up with positive, life-giving energy.

Recall three emotions that were pleasant for you. On an index card, write a short summary of the emotion and the story that facilitated it. Emphasize the positive feeling on the card by accenting it with your own creative flourish. Display the cards in places you can always look to when you need a little help shifting into a more positive state of mind.

JANUARY **25**

Everything Is Relative Meditation

Humans—especially empaths—give a lot of power to their emotions and lose sight of their impermanence. Feeling states are temporary experiences that provide you with information and insight. This is a way to let the feelings come and go, without holding on to them. Sit down in a comfortable position and take a deep inhale, expanding your belly. Begin to check in with your emotional state. Ask yourself, "What emotion is present right now?" Try not to force the experience, but instead allow it to come to you. Once you identify it, imagine seeing it in tangible form—anger, for instance, can look like a dusty cloud covering your body. Then imagine the dust cloud settling, and come back to the breath. Whenever the feeling returns, neutrally note it as "anger," and again visualize the dust cloud settling.

JANUARY **26**

Overcoming Perfectionism

An empath's standards for themselves and their ability to be there for others can be unfeasibly high. This can cause you to come down hard on yourself if you miss an opportunity to offer support. Journal about a similar experience and explore why your response was self-critical instead of understanding.

JANUARY **27**

I Trust Myself

Being overly empathic can sometimes warp your natural intuition. Practice reconnecting with your inner knowing by affirming:

I will honor my inner voice when it advises me to step out of the situation.

JANUARY **28**

Taking Time to Unplug

Whether you spend your days in front of a computer or stay up late swiping through social media, most of us are near constantly plugged in. It's easy to feel flooded by all the stimulation and personalities online. Putting down the gadget is an intentional act, signaling your mind to get out of autopilot and to fill your time creating meaningful moments. Dedicate one hour for the next seven days to completely unplug from any devices and keep them out of reach. Each time, challenge yourself to take a longer break from your devices and the plights associated with technology.

JANUARY 29

Loving-Kindness Meditation

When you offer someone loving-kindness, you send them a wish of goodwill. Empaths do this meaningfully while considering the person's struggles and emotions at the time. However, it can be difficult for them to remember they have no control over this person's experiences and feelings.

For this meditation, select someone in your life to send a well-wish to. It can be a stranger you saw on TV, an acquaintance, or even yourself. Close your eyes and visualize this person. Take three deep breaths and bring your awareness into your heart. Think, or speak, a statement that conveys something you hope they will feel or experience. Start by using the word "may" and follow with the appropriate pronoun: "May you feel lighter in your soul today," or "May they have a day free from pain," for example. Be sure to focus your awareness on the statements as you send them out with warm and caring energy.

JANUARY 30

Resisting Guilt

When you notice guilt or shame in your body, simply say:

It was not wrong to choose myself. I am free to let go of guilt.

JANUARY 31

Knowing When to Disengage

Every now and then, it might feel difficult to engage in a conversation that will expend a lot of empathic energy, but it's in an empath's nature to stay. Perhaps you fear you'd be letting someone down or you've set a precedent as the friend who's always there. Journal about the pros and cons of not acting on your empathic reflexes.

FEBRUARY 1

Setting Negative Thoughts Free

There are many creative ways to help you access a healthy state of mind. Sometimes creating a tangible version of a metaphysical concept can help the brain get over any barriers to understanding.

Grab ten sheets of paper and a marker. On each piece of paper, write in big letters a negative thought that is either a reflection of what you're currently struggling with or a manifestation of a struggle that's been present for a long time. When you're done, crumple up each sheet of paper and toss it in the garbage can. Imagine yourself feeling lighter and lighter with each sheet that's thrown away.

FEBRUARY 2

My Self-Care Is Nonnegotiable

By buying this book, you likely feel called to seek out a more calm, resilient, and mindful mindset. Clearly state for yourself all the reasons why your daily self-care routine is nonnegotiable. Go into detail about how and why it's rewarding for you. Set the intention to honor your body and its care going forward.

FEBRUARY 3

Sensing a Scent Meditation

For this meditation, concentrate on using your sense of smell to keep your focus on the present moment. The scent should be something that you can detect, yet not so overpowering that it is difficult to inhale beyond a few breaths. Light a candle, use an essential oil in a diffuser (lavender can have a calming effect), or sit nearby while someone is cooking. As you breathe in, become aware of any scent your nose picks up, and breathe out slowly with intention. On the next few in-breaths, begin to visualize the scent wafting toward you, and become aware of it as it comes into contact with your nostrils. With each inhale, expand your awareness to include more of your nasal passageway, your sinuses, and your throat. Note any particular qualities of the scent, like a level of sweetness or intensity. When your mind wanders, gently invite it to return to the inhale.

FEBRUARY 4

Reconnecting with Your Inner Child

Life is challenging and often zaps you of much-needed energy. So schedule some playtime to reinvigorate and cultivate a bit of joy. Take a moment to think of a pastime that makes your inner child smile or laugh. Maybe it's something you haven't done in years or haven't tried before. Go to a paint class, learn a new language, take up clay sculpting, learn how to golf, or try baking a new recipe. Play by yourself or with others, at home or outside of it. Whatever you do, be sure to let go and connect with your younger self.

FEBRUARY 5

Keeping a Healthy Distance

As you learn more about your empath self, you'll discover the best way to temper the intensity of your empathic responses. Even so, refusing to take on your partner's feelings might feel impossible because you care so deeply for them. Write about a past relationship that made it hard to keep a healthy emotional distance. How would you respond today?

FEBRUARY 6

Seek Grounding Objects

For this meditation, choose an object that can fit in the palm of your hand. It can be something you already have, or something you find that has little to no meaning. Open one palm and place it in your hand. Close your eyes and take a few grounding breaths as you gently close your fist around it. Bring your awareness to how it feels in your hand—what is its shape? Move it around between your fingers, rub your thumb over it occasionally, and squeeze it in your hand as you allow it to tether you in the present moment. How does it feel against your hand and fingers? Is it cool or warm to the touch? When your mind wanders, gently refocus your attention on an aspect of the object.

FEBRUARY 7

Self-Check-In

Caring for yourself means checking in every so often to see if you're getting what you need. Ask yourself the following questions: "What does fulfillment truly feel and look like to me? Outside of fulfillment in connecting with others, what else gives me a sense of purpose?"

FEBRUARY 8

Find Power in Sensitivity

When you're feeling hurt by having been called out for being too sensitive, choose to repeat this empowering statement:

I am not too sensitive. I am awake.

FEBRUARY 9

Shutting Off Autopilot

Being empathic is a superpower, but it also means that your reflex is to support, listen, and absorb stress and suffering. As you learn to manage your gifts, preventing exhaustion and being mindful in the moment will be crucial. This means sometimes you'll need to disengage your autopilot. Try this: Take a moment to pause, look around you, and identify fifteen objects and their corresponding colors. Take a slow breath before you name each object to bring your awareness from your thinking to your present environment. Repeat two more times. Once you learn how to intentionally return to the present with a nonjudgmental attitude, you will be able to do any activity more mindfully.

FEBRUARY 10

Feel Free

It's common for empaths to feel compelled to nurture and care for those around them. Empaths may even take on struggles that fall outside the scope of their comfort zones. Despite wanting so badly to alleviate someone's suffering, your deeply sensitive and caring soul needs to occasionally be given permission to rest and unburden itself. Closing your eyes, take a deep breath in through your nose, and exhale a longer breath through your mouth. Maintain your attention on the sound of breathing in. Feel the breath enter your nose and flow to the back of your throat. With each out-breath, visualize yourself free from being compelled to help any moment someone needs it. Visualize exhaling feelings of overwhelm. Breathe out slower each time, becoming lighter the longer that you exhale.

FEBRUARY 11

Keep Your Load Light

The next time you feel overwhelmed or burdened, make room for something more fulfilling or reenergizing by affirming:

I now release worry to gain more peace.

FEBRUARY 12

Focus Attention on Yourself

A large part of self-care is learning to give yourself the same attention as you give those around you. Journal about positive emotions you experience that don't involve other people. Maybe it is the joy that your pet brings you or reading a good book. Whatever emotions you write about, make sure they're about you.

FEBRUARY 13

Say No to Perfectionism

Empaths often hold themselves to perfectionistic standards of friendship, believing that there should never be a lapse in the support they provide. Acting differently from what you view to be your identity as a friend sets the stage for negative self-talk. To keep things in perspective, ask a trustworthy friend to give you a list of ten adjectives that describe your empathic personality. Choose to accept their affirmation and make it your truth. Practice repeating the following acceptance statements: "I accept that I am a _____ friend. I accept that no friend is capable of being there all the time."

FEBRUARY 14

Stand Tall

Throughout life, you will come across those who are unable to comprehend your abilities or who are willing to take advantage of your lenient tolerance. Think about a time when you felt the need to shrink yourself and your abilities to accommodate the opinion of another person. How did that experience inform your boundaries today?

FEBRUARY 15

Listen to Your Body

All your life, your body has been your vessel and a source of strength that deserves care and attention. Lie down if you can, or sit in a chair, and keep your feet and palms a comfortable shoulder width apart. As you begin to take deep breaths, draw your awareness to the top of your head. You can imagine it as if you are looking at yourself in a mirror. Take a few breaths and maintain your attention, slowly scanning your forehead, eyes, cheeks, and jaw. Gently note anything you notice—tension or calm—without judgment. You don't have to do anything about any stress you feel yet; just practice making your way down all the parts of your body down to your toes. After your body scan, feel free to come back to a specific part of the body that you want to give extra attention.

FEBRUARY 16

Choose to Play

Not everything has to be serious, painful, or overshadowed by emotion. Remind yourself to find levity when able:

Today, I will be more playful. Today, I will move with a lighthearted spirit.

FEBRUARY 17

Acknowledge the Dark

Journaling is a perfect opportunity to write about some of the feelings that empaths rarely acknowledge within themselves, like frustration, loneliness, exhaustion, and insignificance. In your journal, write about any challenging emotions, past or present, that you experience in any of your relationships with friends, colleagues, or family.

FEBRUARY 18

Do a Social Media Cleanse

Social media provides access to witness countless people's life stories. Although it's often rewarding to an empath to be moved by remarkable human experience, you need breaks from feeling all the feels. Today, carve out ten minutes from your day to go through the accounts or people you follow and take steps to unfollow anyone whose content consistently triggers your nervous system in a negative way. Doing this is an action that is entirely in your control and will signal to your brain that you are willing to create boundaries for yourself and prioritize self-care with regard to life online.

FEBRUARY 19

Show Gratitude to Your Heart

Practicing gratitude for organs that keep you alive is an excellent way to keep a healthy perspective even when everything feels like it's too much to handle all at once. Take your hands and place them over your sternum, sensing your lungs fill with new air. On the exhale, imagine yourself entering your chest cavity and finding your heart—you can see how hard it works to pump blood through your body, keeping you alive. Find a place to sit where you can watch your heart do its beautiful thing: beating steadily, sometimes faster, other times slower. Notice how it provides blood to each organ, ending with the skin, via veins and arteries. Looking up at it with admiration and humility, offer it your sincerest thanks.

FEBRUARY 20

Give Yourself a Break

If today's a day when you're not feeling up to being an empath, empower yourself by saying:

It's okay to take a break from caring about everything and everyone all the time to focus on my self-care.

FEBRUARY 21

Does It Bring Me Joy?

A messy space can exacerbate an already anxious state of mind and body. How stress appears in the energy of someone's space is unique to each person. Maybe it looks like collecting unnecessary items, leaving huge piles of clothes, or cluttered shelves and cabinets. What does it show up as for you?

Identify a part of your space that could use a little TLC. Spend one hour cleaning up the area, approaching it mindfully and without judgment. With each item you put in its place, visualize releasing any stuck mental energy. If you start to feel overwhelmed, remember that this is a changeable situation.

FEBRUARY 22

Manifest Calm Interactions

It's likely that you've experienced interactions with others that were tiring, unpleasant, or painful, but not everyone needs to leave you drained. As you're learning how to better manage your energy expenditure, visualize an interaction that results in little emotional or mental energy loss—like ordering a coffee or asking a salesperson for their opinion. Keep your breath steady as you imagine engaging in an inconsequential or uninteresting conversation or listening to a friend's dating saga that you've heard at least ten times. Notice how your body feels when there's no emotional charge. The key is to focus on the lack of reactivity so that the next time your body tenses up, you can channel the way you feel when your empathy isn't being called upon. When your mind wanders, remember to come back to the stillness and calm in your body.

FEBRUARY 23

Let It Flow

Things often seem obvious until we start writing. Then we realize that there is a world full of possibility that we didn't know we had access to. In your journal or on a sheet of paper, compose a stream-of-consciousness list of anything that gives you energy.

FEBRUARY 24

Soothe Your Heart

Being highly attuned to others' stress and worry goes hand in hand with a highly attuned nervous system. When you start picking up on the tense vibes, whether in a one-on-one conversation or in a bigger group, your brain's fight-or-flight center starts to light up, producing a nervous system response. Once you notice your physiology is going a little haywire, it's the perfect time to practice one type of self-soothing that will activate the care system, which calms your stress response. Place your hand against your chest, directly over your heart—feel the pressure and warmth of your hand as you imagine sending yourself soothing energy.

FEBRUARY 25

Shield Your Mental State

In a moment when someone's intense emotional state is seeping into your mental space, repeat to yourself:

I am not taking this on. I choose to stay in peace. I am not taking this on.

FEBRUARY 26

Enforce the Nonnegotiables

Remember that if your needs aren't met, then it becomes more difficult to support others the way you may want to. In your journal, take time to write about what your nonnegotiable needs are—both individually and in relationships. Are they being met? If not, why?

FEBRUARY 27

Stay in the Present Moment

Mindfulness is a prerequisite to any self-care. It is the practice of purposefully returning to "the now" without judgment. Meditation asks you to return to the present moment, whether you use a mantra, an object, or a movement.

Close your eyes and begin with some deep inhales. Bring your awareness to the content of your mind. When you realize that your mind tries to reexamine an event or plan the future, simply note it for what it is: past or future. In between wandering, remember that "the now" is sitting and breathing. Your mind will wander a lot—that's what minds do. Acknowledge that it has wandered and gently bring your awareness back to the stillness of your body or the feeling of your breath. When you catch your mind getting lost in thought or emotion, keep bringing your attention back to the now.

FEBRUARY 28

A Moment to Heal

Empaths who seek to use their empathic gifts to heal and nurture others often haven't fully healed themselves of past traumas or challenging upbringings. What do you want to heal within yourself? What can you prioritize to become a more mindful empath?

MARCH 1

Dive into Creativity

Staying creative helps empaths battle imbalance, stress, and general discontent. Creativity is about problem-solving with imagination, inventing something, expressing yourself, and sending a message out into the world. In this activity, visit a relative or longtime friend with whom you'd like to connect. Bring a sketch pad and some drawing utensils. Spend some time sketching this person, taking note of their features and overall aura. Use your intuition to inform your drawing. Alternatively, if you're unable to do an in-person visit, consider interviewing them over the phone to write a fun story together, or record their own life story for recordkeeping.

MARCH 2

What Are My Values?

As people-pleasers, empaths often have difficulty establishing boundaries in relationships. To become more comfortable advocating for your emotional and cognitive limits, it's important to connect to your core values. In your journal, write down five fundamental truths that make you *you*. How can you use these values to set firm boundaries in your relationships?

MARCH 3

Move through Heavy Emotions Meditation

This meditation is perfect for when you're exhausted from a conversation, or you've just watched a heavy film. It can help you shift through uncomfortable or difficult feelings.

Keep your eyes closed or open with a soft gaze. After a few deep breaths, bring your awareness inward and notice if an emotion is present and name it. Imagine you were able to physically watch the feeling as it moved through your body and mind. Begin to observe the feeling at a distance, without judgment. Bring your awareness to where you feel it in your body. When you catch yourself thinking, bring your focus back to the feeling in your body. This is an opportunity to build insight, which is a very important part of practicing the kind of self-care that will benefit you not only in the short term, but also the long term as well.

MARCH 4

Stay Clear of Chaos

You will inevitably meet those who seek to draw others, including you, into their chaotic and dramatic moments. You don't have to let them. Affirm:

I am present and caring without investing emotionally.

MARCH 5

Date Yourself

Planning a date night for the one and only *you* is a mindful and sweet way to show love toward yourself. When you practice self-care, you are much better equipped to care for others. Your relationships are healthier, you feel more peaceful, and you are better equipped to regulate your emotions. Drive to check out a beautiful sunset, have a cozy movie night at home, schedule a manicure, or go see your favorite theater play. Choosing to deliberately spend time revisiting the things you love is an amazing gesture of devotion to yourself.

MARCH 6

Sweet Dreams Are Made of This

Today, let your imagination take you to places you've only dreamt of. If you could have the ideal week of rest and recuperation, what would that week look like? In your journal, write as many details as you can think of. Think big!

MARCH 7

Transition from Empathy to Compassion Meditation

You're likely used to the reflex of naturally taking on the pain of others; however, that is unsustainable and often a detriment to your own mental wellness. Compassion allows you to feel *for* another's pain without taking it on. Call to mind an interaction or experience that has been difficult to shake and replay it in vivid detail. Observe what your body does when you recall this empathic exchange. Ask your muscles to relax as you center yourself with deep breaths. Meditate on the following statement: "I accept that helping this situation is not in my control. I release the need to hold the pain and instead simply wish that the other party be free from suffering." Make the statement your own to fit your experience and repeat it with each breath.

MARCH 8

Listen without Reactivity

Because empaths care, they listen. Listening can become tricky when casual chatting with another turns into high-emotion venting. It's in your nature to instinctively want to alleviate others' challenges. In your next conversation with a high-energy person, practice listening to hear—not to respond. Absorbing information this way puts you in the present, lessens the impulse to react or fix, and keeps your nervous system at bay. Use self-talk to remind yourself that just being present is more than enough for those who want to be heard.

MARCH 9

Comfort at Any Age

Learning how to comfort yourself in a manner that you're receptive to is essential to building a self-care habit. Think back on how you comforted yourself when you were a child, preteen, and teen. In your journal, write about how your behaviors and methods for comforting yourself have evolved over time.

MARCH 10

Practicing Compassion

In today's meditation, you will focus on sending compassionate energy to people you like or love. Bring to mind one person you have positive feelings toward as you settle into your meditating posture. Note whether the person is currently struggling, or if you just want to send some caring energy their way. Compassion doesn't keep you hooked on the line of suffering. On the next full breath, rest your awareness on these words: "May they be free from stress today." If there is another statement that is more fitting, be sure to project that sentiment. It's important that it resonates and feels like compassion. When you've caught your mind going to la-la land, repeat the statement. Bring a soft smile to your face as you keep your focus on sending out the warm and light energy toward your chosen person.

MARCH 11

I Am Growing

Take time to recognize your growth as an empath by affirming:

I like who I am growing into. I am not losing anything; I am gaining wisdom through transformation.

MARCH 12

Look over the Details

Constantly fixating on the details of others' verbal and behavioral patterns is one of the quickest ways an empath's energy depletes. As a result, it can be difficult to stop the near-constant analysis. In your journal, write about a time when empathy impacted you in a negative way. How can you learn from that?

MARCH 13

Engage with Creativity

Taking a break from the constant stream of thoughts, feelings, and sensations, to activate your creative mind can do wonders. Think about what type of creating would offer you a sense of freedom, calm, or any other pleasant feeling. Then pick something that you can experiment with without being perfectionistic or aspirational. Head to a store that carries art and craft supplies with an idea or two in mind and wander the aisles for inspiration. Remind yourself that there is no right way to do this. Grab paints, stickers, DIY sets, or T-shirts to tie-dye—whatever you feel inspired to get. Then carve out time to explore your creativity.

MARCH 14

No Apologies

Without a doubt, you will hear comments about empaths being too much, or sometimes you will feel that way yourself. On the days when this is a challenge for you, affirm:

I will not apologize for being myself.

MARCH 15

Meet Others with Grace

Sometimes your feelings meter will spike when you hear about or see a stranger having a difficult time. It can feel particularly challenging if you can do little to nothing to help. With compassion practice, it becomes easier to let go of this emotional ache. Close your eyes and meet your mind in the present moment. Draw your awareness to the feeling of the floor or chair underneath you, holding you up. Imagine the stranger(s) who your heart hurts for and take a slow, soothing inhale. On the out-breath, say: "I wish them less suffering" or "May they find moments of peace." If you notice your body tensing up, give it a dose of calming energy and bring your attention back to the sound of the statement resonating in your mind. Visualize the stranger(s) receiving the kindness sent their way.

MARCH 16

Let Go of Control

Letting go of trying to fix things, or attempting to control or change others' emotional experience, is a critical step in the ongoing process of self-care. Take some time to reflect on what you fear would happen if you let go of these expectations for yourself.

MARCH 17

You Are Your Top Priority

You often put everyone else first. When it's hard to choose you, affirm:

It's okay to prioritize myself. I deserve the same attention and care that I give to others.

MARCH 18

Release Resentment Meditation

Despite your understanding nature, you are not immune to being hurt. There will be times when sadness or resentment builds up against someone who has caused you pain. Find a comfortable seat and orient to the present moment as you visualize a person who has caused you harm. Label any challenging emotions gently. Bring your awareness to your face—particularly the brow and jaw region—is there any furrowing or clenching? Relax your facial muscles and stretch your jaw if you need to. Choose a sentiment to release as compassionate energy—know that it's normal if it's tough to find one. You can try saying: "May they feel the warmth of the sun this week." It doesn't have to be a grand gesture. Start off easy and spend several meditations repeating these wishes and letting them float away like dandelion seeds in the wind.

MARCH 19

Write Your Own Rule Book

You're building new habits in protecting and caring for your empath soul. Good for you! To keep yourself in check, make an Empath's Rule Book to stay accountable. Create a specific list of encouragements or guidelines for your day's interactions. For example, on Mondays, you could make every effort not to engage in any lengthy conversations. On Thursdays, you could implement a texting cutoff time after which you'll no longer respond to messages that contain requests or emotional charges. Get as creative as you can to make it into a fun process to implement these new practices.

MARCH 20

Identify Triggers

When you're automatically picking up on everyone else's inner experience, it's easy to forget that you also have your own, independent of anyone else. In your journal, write about any triggers that tend to set off a chain reaction of negative emotion. How can identifying these triggers be helpful to you in the future?

MARCH 21

Build New Habits

It can be hard to build new habits. Say:

I promise to be patient with myself and remind myself that I'm doing better than I think.

MARCH 22

Show Compassion Toward Yourself

It may be challenging to practice *self*-compassion, but remember that your very nature needs a certain kind of recuperative energy. Being compassionate to yourself looks like noticing your own discomfort or pain and having the desire to alleviate it. Begin with five minutes of deep breathing to soothe your nervous system. Visualize an image of yourself in present day. Notice if any judgmental thoughts pop up questioning whether or not you deserve compassion. Become aware of any feelings of guilt or shame. Label any thoughts as thoughts, and emotions as emotions. Redirect your awareness to the present moment by asking yourself, "What do I need right now?" It never hurts to offer yourself some inner peace. "May I find a little peace today?" works perfectly. Watch the words form in your mind and visualize a peaceful energy filling your heart area.

MARCH 23

Examine Feeling Helpless

As an empath, you may often feel helpless as you realize that some suffering simply cannot be alleviated no matter how much you try to help. In your journal, write about a scenario where you felt helpless in some way. In hindsight, what was in your control and what wasn't?

MARCH 24

Acknowledge Your Superpower

It's important to acknowledge your superpower from time to time because it's not so easy being you. Affirm:

Even though it can be overwhelming, I love the way I listen to others.

MARCH 25

Channel a Mentor

Most of us have met an empath who has mastered the skill of protecting their energy and not taking on the weight of other people's suffering. They can feel things deeply, but it doesn't cause them so much stress or pain that they end up drained on a regular basis. Choose someone you know—or imagine someone—who embodies this ability. Imagine, in detail, what it would be like to experience a stressful situation as them. First, create an artistic interpretation that reflects them and their way of clearing outside energy. Using any chosen art materials and your imagination, depict yourself successfully protecting your own space.

MARCH 26

Pick Your Response

You can choose how you respond when you are over-whelmed. Empower your ability by asking yourself, "What will help me suffer less?" In your journal, write about a time when an experience of pain led to mental anguish. What did you do or what could you have done to lessen the suffering?

MARCH 27

Extend Empathy Inward

It's time to talk about something that's on your mind—with yourself. It is important to take the time to consciously offer yourself what you give to others. Find a seat in front of a mirror, ideally in a position that feels organic and comfortable (e.g., cross-legged or wrapping your arms around your knees). Imagine that you are reenacting what it is typically like when you extend your empathy to someone. This time, the "other person" is your reflection. Reflect on something that you have been stressed about or hurting from and talk about it aloud to your reflection in a comforting, understanding way.

MARCH 28

Enforce Your Boundaries

If someone is attempting to violate your boundaries, hold on to this reminder:

People who are unwilling to respect my boundaries are those who benefit the most from the absence of them.

MARCH 29

Positive Inspiration

Journaling doesn't always have to feel serious or reflective. Today, sit with your journal and write a word that makes you feel warm and fuzzy. Repeat this exercise in the future, compiling a list of feel-good words that you can look at whenever you need to channel more positive and restorative energy.

MARCH 30

Forgive Yourself

You may have been known to be a little hard on yourself from time to time, or to hold your powers of listening and deep understanding to an impossible standard. For today's meditation, set your intention to practice self-forgiveness as you settle into your seat. You can choose a statement for a specific situation but start with the practice of a broader sentiment. You might say: "I forgive myself for not always having the perfect reaction." It may help to lightly hug a pillow in your lap or place a hand over your heart, to connect with a soothing, tender quality. As your awareness floats atop your breath, say your statement in your mind. Imagine each word sounding like a soft press of a piano key—a note for each syllable, perhaps. Return your mind's eye to the "melody" of forgiveness over and over again.

MARCH 31

Living in Acceptance

There are moments when you wish you could take away someone's pain, but you won't be able to. Acceptance is key. Affirm this by saying:

I accept that suffering is a part of the human experience that I cannot control.

APRIL 1

Notice Your Thoughts

Becoming a more mindful empath means being able to better distance yourself from your thoughts. For example, when you begin to worry about a struggling family member, your fight-or-flight center hijacks your brain and causes you to ruminate on all aspects of the stressful situation. Noticing invites you to label a thought as a thought without getting caught up in its meaning. Today, each time you catch yourself in a stream of thinking that begins to overwhelm you, say or write the word "thought" or "thinking" and return to your activity. Engage in this activity repeatedly throughout the day.

APRIL 2

Learn from Your Highs and Lows

As an empath, I sometimes feel exhausted to be myself. Do you feel the same? Do you wish you were different sometimes? Let it out in a journal entry—or five. In your journal, write about any thoughts or feelings you have about wanting to take a break from being you.

APRIL 3

Manage Your Sensitive Nature

Meditating on the intention of cultivating inspiration is a useful practice to counter oncoming burnout. Your brain is wired to maintain high sensitivity, yet living at that high level is not sustainable. First, visualize any inspiration you call upon surrounding you as a continuous wave of dreamy, sparkling glitter. Imagine a light sprinkle of sparkles floating around you as you close your eyes and inhale deeply. With each exhale, slow down your breath even more, resting your awareness right at the parting of your lips. With the next inhale, observe the air becoming more glittery around you—that's your inspiration. If your mind wanders to the nitty-gritty of goal setting or planning, bring your mind back into the glittery stream. Continue inhaling and exhaling the flowing energy of creativity and just enjoy the visualization. Keep this meditation in your empath tool kit as a quick, calming practice to use at the onset of stressful situations, communications, or demanding tasks.

APRIL 4

Encourage Yourself to Be *You*

How you are in the world and around others is entirely your choice. Say:

I invest my time and energy when it feels right for me.

APRIL 5

Rethink How You Communicate Your Empathy

Traditional ways of communicating empathy, such as crying or over-worrying, are depleting and detract from the other person's experience. Instead of showing feeling, take action. Think of an acquaintance whose feelings are easy for you to sense. This person should be someone you regularly see. Choose one thing to *do* for them to help lighten their burden. For example, volunteer to walk their dog, order carryout one night, or offer to pick up some groceries for them. This practice allows you to focus on what *is* within your control, serve another, and feel the reward of helping—all without taxing your emotional resources.

APRIL 6

Prioritize Your Mental Health

Taking care of yourself means paying attention to your mental health—especially when your impulse is to always be present for someone else. Choosing to be present for *you* can be difficult. In your journal, write about a specific time when it was challenging to prioritize your mental wellness. How can this cognizance help you today?

APRIL 7

Accept What Is

Acceptance is the nonjudgmental acknowledgment of what is true in the present moment. It releases any emotional reactivity and ends fighting for a truth that you wish was different. As you close your eyes and bring your body to stillness, reflect on a situation that you cannot change. Note what happens in your body when your emotions begin to swell. Do you get angry or want to hide? Is there heat in your face or tightness in your chest? Envision your chest expanding to accommodate anything and everything that's true, even if the reality sucks. State to yourself, "I accept that this is a reality that I cannot change; however, I have infinite space to hold anything I wish were different." Repeat and bring your awareness back to the expansiveness of the space in your chest cavity. Acceptance is hard, but it is essential to caring for yourself and honoring your reality.

APRIL 8

Manage Your Reactions

With practice, you can control the way your body and mind react to your environment. Affirm:

In each moment, I have the freedom to choose the way I respond.

APRIL 9

Know How to Be There for Yourself

Being a great support system and mindful friend is an important and meaningful role to play in others' lives. If you could have a break from all aspects of that role, however, what three things would you do more of? Write about how these priorities would benefit your daily life.

APRIL 10

Listen to Cathartic Music

This is an activity I recommend doing as much as you possibly can! Find music that allows you to release tension, whether it's your favorite angsty soundtrack from your teenage years or a song that makes you cry in a liberating kind of way. Whatever soundtrack you choose, practice listening to a few songs without doing anything else. See if the music inclines you to move, scream, thrash, or dance—whatever it inspires you to do, be sure that it makes you feel like you've just taken a big deep breath or finished a good workout.

APRIL 11

Encourage a Tranquil Mind

The next time you take time to meditate but notice your mind is very busy, say to yourself:

Tranquil and soothing energy flows through me.

APRIL 12

Take Your Own Advice

Are you better at dishing out good advice than taking it yourself? Because empaths are people-pleasers, they typically deprioritize their personal experiences to be present for the other person. In your journal, write a letter to yourself promoting the value of self-care. Be convincing. Mention what self-care can look like and provide some examples, too.

APRIL 13

Exhale Responsibility

You can support someone without becoming responsible for their state of mind. Remember that the person *experiencing* the emotion is the one accountable for their feelings. As you get settled, rejoice in some much-needed deep inhalations and slow exhalations. Set your intention to the following: "I will let go of the responsibility I feel to take care of everyone's suffering." Spend a few minutes vividly recalling a relationship where you often feel like the cause of the emotionality or like you were obligated to take care of any negative feelings. Bring your attention to any physical sensations that arise. Assign "responsibility" and "freedom" each their own color. On the inhale, see the breath as a light blue—you are breathing in freedom. As you breathe out, see the breath leaving you as a heavy stream of dark purple—you are exhaling responsibility.

APRIL 14

Lean on Your Support System

Your deeply giving nature can create an imbalance in relationships, when others do not recognize how far you go to be there for them. In those moments, remember:

I am deeply loved and appreciated.

APRIL 15

Plant to Heal

Think back to a past news story that was overwhelmingly sad and heavy for you to read. When situations feel painful and unfair, it's difficult for empaths to contain their sadness or devastation. Rather than live with that heaviness, plant some seeds. Whether it's tomatoes for your garden, herbs for your windowsill, or a new tree at a local park, use seed planting to revel in the joy and beauty of mother nature. It won't alleviate all the world's struggles, but knowing you are adding some joy to it will help offset the turmoil empaths tend to internalize.

APRIL 16

Lessons from the Younger You

Have you been a highly sensitive human since your earliest memories? If so, that means you've been attuned to those around you since before you learned how to deal with such a powerful gift. Reflect on this and journal about your younger empathic self. What was it like being you back then?

APRIL 17

Observe Rumination

For this meditation, you will combine several of the skills you have already learned. Locate a quiet space and make yourself comfortable. Turn your attention inward to notice your mind cycling through the same thoughts over and over again. There may be a sensation that your brain is stuck in this cycle. This is rumination. As an empath, you want to be reassured that you're always helpful, and sometimes a conversation may not go as you had planned. Concentrate to bring your focus to your belly and chest, expanding both with your in-breaths. Note any recycled thoughts as "thinking." You can continue being mindful of this even outside of the meditation, simply by catching yourself stuck in the thought cycle and labeling it for what it is instead of indulging in it further.

APRIL 18

Honor Your Body's Abilities

Your body often holds much of what you absorb throughout your days. To honor this, say:

I listen to my body, and I am grateful for everything it is capable of.

APRIL 19

Dote on Yourself

Your brain gets a little hit of dopamine anytime you indulge in a little self-gifting. If you're typically a thrifty spender, set a small budget and make a very intentional purchase of a self-care item that you haven't tried before. Envision yourself using it and observe what feeling it gives you. If you typically talk yourself out of buying things for you, then practice the instant gratification of buying a few self-care products without giving yourself a hard time. An affirmation that sounds like "I deserve this!" wouldn't hurt either. This is a treat-yourself moment and there's no need to overthink it.

APRIL 20

Thank You, Body

Your body has taken on a lot of stress and emotions over the years. Write a letter to your body expressing how you feel about what it has done for you. Make it a love letter, an apology, or an exclamation of deep gratitude.

APRIL 21

Clear Stuck Energy

Sitting outside in the fresh air or at an open window, gently set up for cleansing yourself with a mix of breath and visualization. Take a few breaths just to get the feeling of the cool air drifting into your lungs. Imagine the air you're breathing is being sent directly from a dense forest of trees in a misty rain forest. On the inhale, see the vapors as they travel through your nose, throat, lungs, and into your bloodstream that then carries the oxygen to every part of your body. Imagine that as it envelops every bit of anatomy, it swiftly dissolves and sends away stuck, stressful energy. Allow the cool waves of oxygen to eliminate toxins collected from any unpleasant interactions. On every out-breath, watch the air carrying out with it anything that no longer belongs inside you.

APRIL 22

Change Judgment to Curiosity

Wherever you find yourself today, take five minutes to become curious about your surroundings. Counter any stressful moment by asking yourself questions about what you see. Notice something new about at least five observable things in your vicinity. Engage in nonjudgment—this quality of awareness can help you to redefine any frustrating or unpleasant situation as neutral or interesting. Instead of letting anxiety get to you on a crowded train, for example, wonder about what each passenger does for a living, or guess the names of dogs you pass by. Curiosity is self-care that is available to you 24/7.

APRIL 23

Praise Yourself

You're an empath—that means you have some killer intuition. Validate yourself when you listen to it by saying:

I was right to set that boundary.

APRIL 24

Examine a Leaf Meditation

When you're overidentifying with a particular stressor, it can make your field of focus very small. Connecting to the earth reminds you of the relative insignificance of any emotional or mental turmoil in the grand scheme. A leaf is a wonderful object of meditation because up close, its characteristics evoke a sense of wonder and connect you to the complexities of nature. Hold the leaf in the palm of your hand and note its lightness. Begin to look at it more closely as you observe the details of its veiny network and the point of the stem where it unfurled. Feel its texture with your fingers, noting if it's rough or rubbery. Bring it to your nose and see if you can smell the freshness it absorbed from all the oxygen it breathes. Acknowledge how the leaf connects you to everything else on planet Earth.

APRIL 25

How Do I Accept Help?

Because empaths are usually taking care of others, they often don't give their close ones the same opportunity to provide support. Think about a time when you pushed yourself outside your comfort zone and asked for some kind of support. Explore what was difficult about the experience, as well as what may have been helpful.

APRIL 26

Keep Sight of Your Value

When your gifts are dedicated to helping and feeling others, it's easier to lose sight of important and interesting things about you. Say:

My value is not tied to my empathic nature. I am worthy for simply being me.

APRIL 27

Allow Others to Care for You

I'm willing to bet that you have frequently turned down offers of support or care for you, but accepting help or attention doesn't negate your empathic ways. Today, pick a close person(s) who has at some point offered or tried to take care of you even though you ultimately resisted. Choose a way to thank them for their kindness (buy them a cup of coffee or write a thank-you note, for instance) and mention that next time you will practice accepting their proposal to be there for you. Expressing gratitude and an intention to willingly receive support is an act of self-care.

APRIL 28

Tune In to Nature

Find yourself a comfortable spot among the trees, in the grass, or near a stream. Once you've settled in, close your eyes, and begin to bring your awareness to any sounds that are entering your ear. If you pay close attention, you can even catch the sound wave as it hits the entry to your ear canal. Do not search for the sounds, but rather let them come and go as they do. What do you hear? The sound of leaves rustling? The trickle of a babbling brook? The quiet found only on the peak of a mountain? When your mind wanders, practice asking yourself, "What am I hearing right now?" Allow your attention to settle on one sound in particular and observe how it changes as it reaches you. Is it growing louder or softer? Continue your practice by maintaining a gentle awareness of nature's melody.

APRIL **29**

The Power to Change

There may be moments when you realize how acutely you feel everything and how isolating that can be. Empower yourself:

I choose to surround myself with like-minded and like-hearted individuals.

APRIL **30**

Rid Your Bubble of Negative Energy

Caring for yourself means performing routine internal housecleaning, eradicating all types of negative energy from your bubble. Take a moment to recall a conversation where it was difficult to connect with someone because they so obviously lacked empathy. In your journal, write about how that person—or others like them—make you feel in this world.

MAY 1

Make Use of Code Words

Many individuals are under the notion that empaths are constantly available and eager to remain supportive in any situation. As skilled as you are in doing so, you may struggle to let others know when you need a breather. Others should support your need to take a break, but it can be discomforting to know your absence is letting someone down. Take a moment of intention to create a code word you can use with family and friends when you're only available for *you*—not another. Share that with those in your life as a way to enforce your empath boundaries.

MAY 2

Focus on Sound

If you're able to find a small singing bowl for this practice, that's fantastic! If not, pull up a YouTube video or a music app and type in "sound of gong." The sound should be a gentle ringing of a gong, bell, or singing bowl that repeats every ten to fifteen seconds. Sitting comfortably, begin to bring awareness inside your body, letting go of any sounds around you as you breathe in and out. At the next sound of the instrument, take a deep breath in, and slowly let it out through your nose, trying to stay with the pace of the echoing, bright sound. Bring your awareness to the vibrations it creates and imagine that your attention could ride the waves of sound as it dissipates into the quiet. Every time it rings out, do your best to stay present with the emanating sound.

MAY 3

Freewriting

With your journal and favorite pen in hand, find a cozy place to write. Take a deep breath in and release it slowly. Write freely for twenty minutes about what has been weighing on your heart and mind as of late. Feel encouraged to write about every feeling you've experienced; all is valuable here.

MAY 4

Reality Entertainment

Sometimes reality television—of the uplifting kind—can be an effective way to decompress from everyday energy depletion and burnout. It allows empaths to observe people without connecting to them, to become audience members instead of serving as active participants. Whether you choose to watch a wacky family, a British baking show, or some ice road truckers, enjoy the feeling of tuning into an episode (or five) and tuning out of your overworked empathic mind.

MAY 5

Attract Joy

It might feel rewarding to be sought out by those in need, but remind yourself to be careful of the energies you take on:

I attract energies and situations that fill me with joy.

MAY 6

Your Empath Résumé

This book will guide you through creating an elevated self-care plan that builds on what you have done so far. Think about your self-care habits in the past. When you became mindful of your self-care needs, what did you first try? What has and hasn't worked since then? Be thorough!

MAY 7

Facial Presence

As a primary communicator of your inner experience, your face holds a lot of tension at the end of each day. In this practice, you will focus on the muscles and movements within your face. Close your eyes and mentally scan the various parts of your face. Then slowly brush your fingers over your forehead, temples, eyes, nose, cheeks, jaw, lips, and chin. Breathing in, bring your awareness to your forehead. Is it tense or furrowed? On the exhale, release any remaining tension. Next, bring your attention to your jaw. Have you been clenching or grinding? Open your mouth wide and stretch your jaw. Feel the muscles pulling and releasing any residual tightness. On your next inhale, observe your eyes and the surrounding area. Note any sensations of fatigue, straining, or dryness. Gently stroke your closed eyelids as though giving your eyes a massage.

MAY 8

Strength Is My Middle Name

Sensitivity and emotionality are sometimes looked at as "weak" qualities; however, they are anything but. Claim the opposite:

I feel and I am fierce.

MAY 9

Form Your Support Team

Empaths frequently play the role of armchair therapist, but a huge gesture of self-care is counseling the self. Just like during recess as an adolescent, it's time to "pick your team" and form the best support system you can have—all at your choosing. Spend some time online to gather a collection of sources that you know can provide you with emotional and therapeutic support when you need it most. Some sources to consider are supportive friendships, talk therapy, journaling, finding online text support, reading research, or making art. Try to build a team of six to eight support sources to lean back on during challenging empathic moments.

MAY 10

Laugh Therapy

You can reduce the negative impacts that come with taking on people's emotional states by tickling your funny bone. In your journal, recall the funniest thing that's ever happened to you. It could be a recent story or years old, among strangers or alongside loved ones. All that matters is that it makes you laugh out loud.

MAY 11

Sand Timer Meditation

Find a sand timer or pull up a video of one you can watch easily. Sit in a comfortable position, placing the timer at eye level. Taking a deep breath in, flip the timer so that the small pebbles of sand begin to fall through the narrow center. Your present awareness should rest gently on the falling sand as it moves its way from top to bottom. Make sure you're not holding your breath or tensing your body in an effort to pay close attention—this needn't be a struggle. Maintain your breathing at a smooth and relaxing pace. If you catch your mind or eyes beginning to wander, bring your awareness and soft gaze back to the collection of pebbles slipping through the narrow opening and falling to stillness at the bottom of the timer. Continue the practice until all the sand settles.

MAY 12

Celebrate Your Ability

Empaths may feel a lot, but they have every ability to control it. Be sure to assert and celebrate your epic empath qualities and rid yourself of any self-doubt:

I am perceptive. I am insightful. I am patient. I make people feel heard.

MAY 13

Stand Tall

Not everyone comprehends an empath's abilities, which makes it difficult for the empath to feel like they are understood. It's possible for empaths to feel shorted because of the isolation they endure. In your journal, write about what you wish others could more often acknowledge and keep in mind about your empathic nature.

MAY 14

Make a Space

Designating a physical space devoted entirely to meditation and mindfulness practice can function as an at-home retreat. Pick a relatively undisturbed spot in your home where you can envision looking forward to arriving every day. This is where you can keep your pouf, yoga mat, blankets, or comfy chair—whatever you use for your practice. Decorate the space as much as you'd like with soothing colors, objects, scents, or mementos that convey peaceful, healing elements. Have fun coming up with a creative name that you can use to refer to it. Choose to return to and rest in your new space after you've set it up.

MAY 15

Imagination Fun

Making use of your creativity and imagination is a fun way to care for a weary soul. Today, take fifteen minutes to consider and journal about the following: If you wrote a book, what would it be about? Get detailed!

MAY 16

A Shower Meditation

During your next shower, start by mindfully turning the faucet. Use your fingers to feel the water temperature, noting the moment the stream hits your hand. Step in slowly, paying attention to each movement. Alternate between having your eyes closed and open. Before reaching for any of your products, take a minute to let the water hit the top of your head and feel it splash over your shoulders. When your mind wanders, gently bring your attention to the sensations that your body feels. What is the temperature and pressure of the water? Try to catch one stream trickling all the way down over your knees and onto your feet. As you shower, continue to shift your body around to change up where your attention goes (e.g., bending over to let the water splash over your back). Note any judgments that may arise and let them go.

MAY 17

Live in Authenticity

Not everyone is able to understand what it's like to be in someone else's shoes. Some may even expect you to show a lack of empathy. Ignore them:

I will continue to be true to myself.

MAY 18

Delegate Responsibility

In a friend or family group, empaths tend to take on any emotional labor while making every effort to assure everyone has all their other needs met, too. Every person in a group contributes in a unique way to maintain cohesion and connection. For the next week, practice letting others take the reins on actions you normally take. Mutually decide on a different person within the group that can step up and be the go-to. It may be challenging to let go of some of the roles you play, but remember why it's important to practice stepping back from time to time.

MAY 19

Stay Energized

Some days, you may feel too tired or overwhelmed to continue with your day, even though you must. In those moments, say aloud:

I have an abundance of what I need to make it through today.

MAY 20

Blow Bubbles Meditation

Visit your nearest dollar store or big box store and pick up a few packs of bubbles. (Or you can make your own using dish soap.) Then find somewhere you won't be disturbed and where you can blow bubbles to your heart's content. Keeping your eyes open, sit or stand comfortably. As you take a deep breath in, bring the wand to your lips. On the out-breath, bring your attention to the pursing of your lips as you push out air slowly, attempting to create a soap bubble. Use your available senses to identify what you see, smell, touch, hear . . . and taste. (Sometimes soap gets in your mouth!) Try to time your focus so that every out-breath produces a bubble. Bring your attention to any fully formed bubbles and watch them float away.

MAY 21

To Forgive or Forget

You might give everyone the benefit of the doubt because you have an intuitive understanding of what it means to be human. Or you may do it to try to avoid a potentially unpleasant reaction. In your journal, write about an experience where you feared what might happen if you withdrew from responding empathically.

MAY 22

Watch a Flame Meditation

Find a candle and set it in front of you while you sit comfortably in a quiet space. Light the candle and begin to settle in, taking a few deep breaths. Bring your gaze to the flame, then slowly take a deep breath in and out. Observe how the fire flickers and dances, imagining it were putting you into a deep, restful trance. If you're comfortable, move the candle in a little closer so that you can begin to feel the emanating heat. Rest your awareness on where the sensation of warmth hits your body. When your mind wanders, gently guide your gaze back to the flame. Envision that this bit of fire is yours to keep—it represents the empowering energy that you will cultivate as long as you take care of yourself.

MAY **23**

Call the Shots

Take responsibility for your choices to alleviate some of your own suffering. Acknowledge what you can do:

I am able to shift to a calm energy at any point I choose.

MAY **24**

Don't Forget to Pause

Stop what you're doing and take a deep breath in for four counts, then exhale for four more. Ask yourself, "What do I need in this very moment? What do I need at the end of today? What might I need at the end of the week?" Record your answers in your journal.

MAY 25

Practice Saying No

When approached by another with a need, people-pleaser empaths typically sign on for the task straightaway. To maintain good mental and emotional health, protecting their boundaries is something empaths must do for the long term. "No" is always an option for an answer. For this activity, look at yourself in the mirror for ten minutes. Watch yourself say, "No, thank you," over and over again. Look at yourself with a friendly and kind gaze. Accept yourself as a person who has the ability to turn down requests, needs, invitations, and so on. You don't need a justification to practice boundaries.

MAY 26

Anxiety Alleviation Meditation

It's easy to believe that there is no escaping anxiety when you are used to being stuck in an anxious state of mind and body. Fortunately, there are ways to combat it. Set an intention to lower your anxiety as you sit down for today's practice. You can do this before a high-pressure situation or as you notice some anxiety coming on. Notice the stillness in your body. As you breathe in, bring any of the following statements to mind: "I am very calm. I am so deeply relaxed. I am serene. I am peaceful." As you repeat the words to yourself, visualize what it feels like when your anxiety is at its lowest. Picture what your body feels like and how quiet your mind tends to be. Continue to take full breaths and affirm your ability to achieve a relaxed state.

MAY 27

What Will I Release Today?

What will you release today? What will you gain? Affirm:

I release negative self-talk to gain an empowered inner voice.

MAY 28

My Journey with Self-Awareness

As you cultivate your self-awareness, directing your energy toward the right sources and recipients will become easier. In your journal, recall the time when you first noticed your heightened self-awareness. Take yourself on the journey from that moment until now. What areas of self-growth would you like to pay more attention to, and why?

MAY 29

Offer Physical Self-Compassion

Self-compassion involves responding in the same supportive and understanding way you would with a loved one or close friend when you have a difficult time, fail, or notice something you don't like about yourself. It is a prerequisite to any self-care technique. To practice directing your compassion toward your body and nervous system, place a hand over your heart to activate the body's care system, which combats the stress response. Take three big, mindful breaths. Feel the warmth and pressure of your palm against your chest. Mentally send yourself loving and compassionate energy. This is an invaluable tool to use when you sense yourself feeling down.

MAY 30

Thoughts on a Stream Meditation

Consider using this visualization method when you want to help your mind release or let go of a thought. Find a quiet space and get into a comfortable position. Take a few very slow, full inhales, drawing your mind's eye to the ripple of thoughts that are present. Notice how one thought comes right after the other, sometimes too quickly for you to even notice each one as it arrives. As you notice that you are thinking, visualize a trickling stream in the middle of lush, green valleys. When you catch yourself having a thought, imagine that you could pick it up and rest it on one of the leaves. Do the same to each subsequent interruptive thought, watching your thoughts as they drift away from you.

MAY 31

Reject Harsh Energies

When in contact with an energy-draining person, activate your boundaries:

I invite all good and healthy energies into my life. My boundaries protect me from any attempts to influence my emotional state.

JUNE 1

Mindful Plant Care

Most humans rush through activities instead of slowing down to soak up the enjoyment of working on a simple task. Make time to disengage your autopilot. If you have a home filled with greenery, grab your watering can and get ready to do a little mindful caretaking. If not, offer to water the plants at a friend's or family member's place. Move with intention and spend a few minutes with each plant, observing the patterns of the leaves. As you water the thirsty soil, listen for the subtle sound of the dirt soaking it up, and imagine the appreciation of the plant.

JUNE 2

Disengage When Necessary

Sometimes empaths prefer to stay plugged into others' stories and end up avoiding their own. What has your personal experience been with unconscious or conscious avoidance of the stresses in your life? Does being there for everyone else give you a good reason not to be there for something you're going through?

JUNE 3

Listen to a Podcast

Podcasts are stories with a built-in boundary in that you are neither near nor familiar with the storyteller or the characters of the story (and if you miraculously are, consider choosing another podcast). There won't be pressure to answer, to validate, to be present with your entire being, or to soak up any exhausting vibes. You are able to be an audience member without the burden of expectations. Your ears can listen, all while you rest, knowing that you don't have to be anything for anyone. Sure, you'll feel a thing or two depending on the content, but it will naturally allow you to practice being an objective listener.

JUNE 4

Understand Your Limits

There will be times when you will want to do more and it will simply not be possible. Instead, use the following self-talk:

I focus on what I can control and release what I cannot.

JUNE 5

How Can I Support Myself?

When you set a precedent as a person who puts others' emotional needs above your own, even well-meaning people may take advantage of your willingness to give without expectation. Imagine that you could empower yourself this very moment and advocate for yourself as only human, not to be idealized. What might you say?

JUNE 6

Smiling Meditation

If you smile for a minute, your brain will start to believe that you are experiencing a state of happiness and will behave more like it. Give it a try, whether you're already in a good state of mind or not. Begin by opening and gently stretching your jaw and mouth, paying attention to how the muscles feel. Notice what happens when your mouth is neutral. Continue the process by mentally scanning your face, beginning to turn the corners of your mouth up and slowly break into a soft smile. Maintain the smile on your face while taking six deep breaths. Observe if anything begins to change as you continue pulling your face into an even bigger smile. Continue for six additional deep breaths, and then release. How do you feel?

JUNE 7

Relax During an Evening Ritual

An evening self-care routine should be simple, inviting, and low stress. The goal is to end your day with lower levels of emotional and mental stress. Create a ritual that is between five to twenty minutes long. It can consist of smaller activities like a breathing exercise, a mindful skin-care routine, or winding down with some hot tea and stretching. Write it down and hang it in your bathroom as a reminder. It helps to have a set time in order to build the ritual into a habit. Eventually, it will become a reflexive evening practice to recuperate from a tiring day.

JUNE 8

Practicing Gratitude

Self-care can simply be sharing your appreciation for those who support you as you are. Affirm:

I am grateful for the people in my life who show loving-kindness toward me.

JUNE 9

Streaming Light Meditation

This meditation will help you in manifesting a sense of inner stability. Having tangible objects that you can tether your breath to is a powerful way to transform abstract thought into more concrete action. Find somewhere quiet and sit or stand comfortably. With your first breath in, send an empowering energy through your body, rooting you in your strength. On your inhale, imagine a warm, glowing stream of liquid light pouring from the sky and traveling through the top of your head and filling up your extremities. Your present moment is connected to this liquid light. When you return your wandering mind, visualize your body filling up with this warmth and eventually flowing all the way down into and around the core of the earth. As you breathe out, imagine the light coming back up through the ground into your body, securing a steady internal energy.

JUNE 10

Reflect on Rest

When you take time for yourself to rest and recharge, how do you feel afterward? In your journal, write about the benefits of setting aside some "me" time. If you could add one self-care action to the time you take for yourself, what would it be?

JUNE 11

Hold Space for Others

Allow yourself to care for someone who is in discomfort without offering an emotional connection. Affirm:

I accept that conflicting feelings often happen at once. They are not mutually exclusive.

JUNE 12

Face Washing Meditation

Coupling meditation practice with an activity you typically engage in is a great way to build a new mindfulness habit. The next time you do your skin routine, whether it's just splashing water on your face or a step-by-step cream-and-serum regimen, find a comfortable stance in front of the sink. Do your best not to glance in the mirror before you turn on the faucet and set the temperature by holding your hand underneath the running water. Fill your cupped hands and bring them to your face, observing the drops of water as they roll down your cheeks and chin. Move with intention as you guide any other liquid to your skin-care routine. Massage any oils or serums with a circular motion, being mindful of the texture against your cheeks and forehead.

JUNE 13

Complete a Simple Task

Humans often set lofty goals and become quite disappointed when they don't reach them. The reality is that there is a feeling of success even in the smallest of tasks—like matching up the socks from your pile of laundry, doing dishes, or watering your plants. Reserve an hour or so for finishing a simple chore. Whether you decide to build a new bookshelf you ordered or change all your bedding, do your best to move mindfully. This means not rushing through a task; instead, intentionally bask in the simplicity and success of whatever you're getting done.

JUNE 14

I Am Worthy

You are worthy of the same care you give to others. Support that by stating:

I deserve to take the time and intentionally take care of myself.

JUNE 15

With Whom Do I Surround Myself?

Your friends and loved ones are cherished, but so are your boundaries. Set aside fifteen minutes to reflect on and journal about the following questions: Do people you surround yourself with lift you up or bring you down? Is there someone with whom it's more difficult to set boundaries?

JUNE 16

Reread a Favorite Book

There's nothing like finding refuge in reliable sources of comfort. Even if you're already a voracious reader, make time to find a book that doesn't require you to pay the close attention you do when reading a brand-new story. Reading allows you to escape to other worlds, forgoing both screens and real-life empath struggles. When you go looking for your book of choice, consider picking up a familiar children's book for a nostalgic throwback, or read a classic that you haven't dusted off in years. Whichever genre you choose, make sure your mind and soul can find retreat.

JUNE 17

Beat Overwhelming Moments

If your mind is plagued with overwhelming thoughts of concern or sadness, affirm:

I respect my inclination to care for others. My strength helps me release unhealthy thoughts that are not mine.

JUNE 18

Mantra Meditation

A mantra is a word or phrase that carries a meaning unique to you, and it can help with motivation and manifestation. Choose an affirmation that speaks to you or come up with your own mantra that makes you move toward a more powerful, positive state. Try to keep it fairly short so that you have no trouble remembering it during the meditation. Sit in an upright position with a straight spine. You can start with the following empowered line good for any empath: "I'm not taking this on." This can refer to any stress, emotion, or burden that you would like to have a boundary against. On every inhale, envision yourself in an empowered state, and with every exhale, say firmly to yourself, "I'm not taking this on." You can change your mantra to reflect the state of mind you are trying to achieve.

JUNE 19

Become Your Protector

Being a deep feeler often correlates with being a chronic helper. That's why it's vital to know your limits and honor them in your day-to-day routines. To further examine your boundaries, answer the following: I shield myself from energy drainers by _____.

JUNE 20

Observe over Absorb

Your mind's reflex is to mirror people's inner and outer experiences and to absorb them. In order to create an invisible barrier between your energy field and that of others, you have to become comfortable in observer mode. Imagine a realistic situation that typically sets off your empathic radar. Write down the positive or negative effects of absorbing the energy of the situation in your journal. Next, imagine that you are an investigator wanting to collect data for later examination. As you recall the details, list anything you objectively observe without adding any opinions or emotional reactions. Compare and contrast the effects of absorbing and observing.

JUNE 21

I'm Allowed to Feel

If you place pressure on yourself to be there for everyone's issues and you've gotten used to letting the negativity fester, give yourself permission to release. Affirm:

I reclaim the space that is mine.

JUNE 22

Cultivate Mental Clarity

If you're feeling overstimulated or overwhelmed, this is a great practice to keep in your bag of self-care tricks. Sit in a comfortable position where you can rest your arms in your lap, palms facing up. Close your eyes, or keep them open. Focus on the tips of your fingers and inhale, one hand at a time. On the exhale, touch your thumb to index finger, thumb to middle finger, thumb to ring finger, thumb to pinkie finger, and back in the other direction. Rest your attention on the sensation of touching finger pad to finger pad. Change up the speed and pressure that you use. Take breaks by relaxing your hand and the fingers.

JUNE 23

Examine Depletions

Many empaths benefit from balancing energy-draining moments with moments of rest. Recall a day or moment from the last week when you felt overwhelmingly tired. Note *why* you felt particularly depleted and who, or what, caused it. Did you feel drained at once, or over time? Be detailed.

JUNE 24

Stretch for Tension Relief

Do you feel better after a deep stretch? Stretching is a simple action that has huge rewards for your body and spirit. The tension and stress that you accumulate over numerous daily encounters gets absorbed by your body. The energy you absorb from others not only swirls around in your mind, but it makes a home in your body, too. Your muscles and ligaments can become tight and painful due to your sensitive nature. This makes stretching even more important for empaths—it's an opportunity to release literal pockets of trapped, embodied suffering. Locate what parts of your body feel tight—is it in the lower back, shoulder-to-neck area, or jaw? Give them a stretch!

JUNE 25

Travel Visualization

Sometimes the only way to get out of your head is to stay in it. Envision going anywhere else in the world. Let your mind be free to imagine you are a traveler going from place to place in your mind. Choose anywhere that you want to go and be specific with the details of the setting as you meditate. Do you see the ocean, tall grass, a dirt road, grove of olive trees, or flock of birds? Do you hear anything? The sound of a crackling fire or a warm wind in Tuscany? When your mind wanders, let your mind walk back over to your chosen location. Focus on what your five senses experience in the visualization. Imagine what the hot sand feels like against your feet. Smell the fresh-roasted Italian coffee. Taste the salt of the ocean as you take a dip.

JUNE 26

Empathy and Boundaries

Being empathic does not mean you are committed to taking on others' burdens; that's what boundaries are for. You get to choose! Say aloud:

I hold both empathy and boundaries in my heart at the same time.

JUNE 27

Practice Self-Love

Self-love is self-care. You might frequently hear the phrase and guidance but aren't great about putting it into practice. Set aside fifteen minutes to journal about at least five aspects of yourself that you can give more love and self-care to.

JUNE 28

Animal Nurture

Animals have a remarkable ability to reduce stress and bring joy—just by being themselves. Aside from having their basic needs met, they do not expect anything else of you, which is a true gift. If you or someone you know has a pup, cat, lizard, or tweeting bird, or if you can visit or volunteer at a shelter, this is easily one of the best ways to give your attention without losing your energy. Once with the animal, choose to intentionally spend some positive and mindful time petting, feeding, and observing them. Refill your energy reserves by connecting with a different species.

JUNE 29

Coulda, Woulda, Shoulda

It's easy to get caught up in the past when you are a self-reflective being. You might find yourself reliving moments where you "could have" done or said something differently. Is there anything on your mind that you've had trouble letting go? Write about what it would take for you to stop reliving the past.

JUNE **30**

Let It Be

Some days are more challenging than others, but all have stressful components. At the end of each day, practice saying aloud:

I release any anxieties and stresses of my day.

JULY **1**

Explore Pleasure Meditation

If you spend most of your time wrapped up in various energy-depleting exchanges, you may be out of practice or have trouble focusing when it comes to cultivating moments of pleasure. Pleasure can range from physical to sexual to mental. Lie down or sit with your back against a wall, with arms at your sides. As you close your eyes, what images come to mind when you think of "pleasure"? Spend some time breathing slowly and daydreaming. Choose a scenario that naturally evokes an enjoyable sensation and begin to visualize it very vividly, as if you were going through the details of each frame of a film. Pause every so often to notice how your body and mind respond as you meditate on the sensation of pleasure. Do you catch yourself smiling or giggling? Do you notice a sensation of longing? Acknowledge any feelings as they arise.

JULY 2

Lead as an Empath

You deserve to feel as supported and empowered as you make others feel. Set aside ten to fifteen minutes to journal about what empowers you. What makes you feel strong enough to walk through life as an empath?

JULY 3

Have Fun with Aromatherapy

Empaths truly benefit from nature. Essential oils, one of the most popular tools in self-care, are compounds extracted from plants with special properties. Some of the most useful essential oils are juniper, which stimulates and strengthens nerves; lavender, which calms and uplifts; and lemon, which cools and abates anger. In this activity, make an essential oil sensory bucket. Grab a bucket or tub and fill it halfway with water. Add fun water beads to change the color of the water. Include colorful gems, too! Don't forget to add a few drops of the essential oil. Let your inner child play—and your nose enjoy the fragrance.

JULY 4

Inhale Peace

When stuck in a situation in which you're interacting with someone who is very negative, don't participate in their toxic energy. Take a few breaths and say:

I inhale peace and exhale negativity.

JULY 5

Lighten the Load

Letting go of certain behaviors and beliefs—like worrying about what others think of you or always trying to make everyone happy—can lighten your spirit. It will take intention and practice. Make a list of things that are holding you back, or weighing you down, that you would like to release.

JULY 6

Delay a Response

Empaths are often responsive texters due to their wish not to leave anyone hanging. However, it gets tiring to maintain the different conversations, especially if they are emotionally charged and require your presence. This week, consciously make the decision to text back at a more leisurely pace than usual. Trust in your ability to know which texts can be left unread for a while, and use reaffirming self-talk to feel reassured that you are not letting anyone down by delaying a response. Catch yourself reaching for the phone to check notifications and practice sitting with the discomfort of not responding straightaway.

JULY 7

Heal Your Wounds Meditation

This is a helpful meditation to practice when you're feeling hurt but don't want to open up to someone else about it. Once settled into stillness, recall an event that harmed you. As you replay the moments, notice if any potent emotion arises and causes any discomfort. What did you feel when the hurt first happened? Visualize that experience as if it were a tangible wound on your body. Where would you find it? Is it a new scar? A small incision? A gaping hole? Explore your inner landscape as you recall any details of the pain you felt. Then imagine pouring a magical concoction that stimulates healing over it. Continue to observe any fluctuations in your emotional state.

JULY 8

Self-Check-In

Every day is a good day to check in with yourself. Set aside ten minutes to journal a self-check-in today, reflecting on and answering the following questions: How is my energy level? How has my boundary setting been lately?

JULY 9

Observe, Not Participate

When in the presence of a disagreement or argument, empaths most assuredly want to help resolve it. Protect your energy by affirming:

I detach from the drama that surrounds me.

JULY 10

Witness the Stars

Mindfully gazing up at a starry night is a magical experience. For this activity, grab a blanket and head into your backyard or other nearby outdoor space. Lie down and observe the sky. Note which stars burn the brightest and see what shapes you can make by connecting the dots. See if you can spot any phenomena, or any stars you find particular interest in. Imagine yourself perched atop a star, seeing how tiny and insignificant your worries are back on planet Earth. Alternatively, search for a sky chart or constellation map online to stargaze in the comfort of your own home.

JULY 11

Feel the Heat Meditation

Choose a day this week when you can sit or lie down comfortably outside, settling in before the cooler, late-morning sun turns into a hot afternoon. The rising temperature will be your object of focus as you close your eyes and become aware of your body coming into contact with the heat. Visualize the bright, scorching sun enveloping you as it approaches its highest point in the day. Pay attention to the sensation of the rays beating against your skin and note any humidity in the air. Bring your awareness to the moment you inhale the hot air. Every five minutes, mentally scan your body and acknowledge any sensations, such as a change in temperature. Are you accepting or resisting the rising heat?

JULY 12

Take a Break

Think back to the last time you took a genuine break from your daily routine. Fantasize about a trip or vacation you could take that would require little to no energy or resources on your part. In your journal, write about it in detail for ten to fifteen minutes. Be creative and dream big!

JULY 13

Focus on Wellness

Too many restorative wellness activities, too little time. If you're comfortable with a light splurge, choose an activity out of the following: facial, acupuncture, or massage. If you find yourself putting off scheduling something that is explicitly for *you*, this is your opportunity to do it. Put everything else aside and get yourself an appointment with an expert who will take care of you. Acupuncture, in particular, is a wonderful activity to schedule at regular intervals, as it has a cumulative benefit for everything from relief of pain to help with sleep cycles.

JULY 14

Acknowledge Your Limits

It's challenging to stay uplifted about the world once burnout happens. Regain positivity by affirming:

When I look at the world as a good, happy, and kind place, good, happy, and kind things come to me.

JULY 15

Live an Authentic Life

An empath has their own unique purpose and way in which they serve others. When you connect to your purpose, it's easier to know how to live more authentically. Shine your light for all to see, dear empath. Yes, be kind, compassionate, and considerate, but not at the expense of your authenticity. Take a few moments to think about your authentic self. How would you describe it? Write that down. When do you feel the most authentic? Do you feel your authenticity is always welcomed? How do you combat that? Write that down, too.

JULY 16

Warm Water Meditation

Everything changes, including moods, patterns of thought, and states of mind. Instead of fighting it, you can practice observing and embracing it. Turn on a faucet so that the water runs warm. Fill up the bottom of a bathtub or a big container that can fit both your feet. Close your eyes and bring your toes to the top of the water. Note how they feel before you slowly submerge them and observe the way the warm water impacts each part of your foot. Notice your feet relaxing as they sink to the bottom, immersed in the warmth. Take your feet out and notice how the air hits them. Submerge them again for ten minutes, always bringing your wandering mind back to your feet. At some point, you will observe the cooling of the water. Did you catch the moment the temperature changed?

JULY 17

Incorporate Meaningful Rest

The next time you're feeling a little sleepy or simply craving to be horizontal for a bit, don't talk yourself out of it. You deserve some intentional rest. It becomes a reflex to come up with reasons why you're too busy or shouldn't get a little shut-eye midday, but this is your chance to practice putting everything else aside and resting your head for a bit. Grab your coziest blanket, set a timer if you must, give yourself permission to check for holes in your eyelids, and let your eyes flutter closed. If it is helpful, imagine being a child in daycare getting to rest midday in a dark, sleepy room.

JULY 18

Positive Reinforcement

It's important to give yourself positive reinforcement when you practice self-care. Affirm:

I feel lighter and recharged, and I will carry this feeling throughout my week.

JULY 19

Release Suffering Meditation

Find a quiet spot you can sit or stand comfortably for today's practice. With intention, send the air you inhale through your body down to your toes. Check in with yourself: What has been causing you discomfort or suffering this week? Choose one thing to focus your attention on. On your next inhale, bring your arms up slowly until they are above your head. On the exhale, let out a groan, yawn, moan, or any other sound that comes to you. Completely relax your body, bending forward or relaxing against a wall or back of a chair. Attempt to feel the relaxing feeling all the way to your fingertips and toes. Repeat the motions for each set of breaths, each time letting out an uninhibited sound, imagining that it carries away any stress you may have inside you.

JULY **20**

My Self-Care Ritual

As an empath, you've probably heard every suggestion in the book, from drinking more water to getting better sleep to exercising. First, list the self-care practices that have worked for you. Then jot down some of the practices that are constantly suggested to you because you're an empath—but just seem to miss the mark.

JULY **21**

Take in Some Comedy

Laughter *is* the best medicine, thanks to the release of some feel-good chemicals that lower stress levels. Commit the next week to weaving in some form of comedy throughout each of your days. When working, take a break every one to two hours to watch some hilarious videos of people or animals doing funny or ridiculous things. Plan a dinner with a friend who cracks you up, and tune in to an audio recording of your favorite comedian's stand-up special on your commute home. Every evening, scroll through the comedy genre of a streaming service to pick a movie that will make you LOL.

JULY 22

I Come First

It is okay to put yourself first. Affirm that today:

I will prioritize my needs by nourishing my body, mind, and soul.

JULY 23

Sink into Stillness Meditation

When the norm is a busy mind, stillness is self-care. However, it is a particular challenge for someone whose mind has a tendency to fixate on the past or future—which is nearly every human. Settle into your most comfortable upright position and fill your body with air on the inhale, down to your toes. Spend a few moments transitioning awareness from the outer world to your inner world. What images come to mind when you think of busyness and stillness, respectively? Observe the different qualities between the two, paying particular attention to how the thought of each affects your body and mind. Imagine you are a tangled clump of sea moss being tossed back into the ocean. Use your breathing to ground you as you visualize peacefully drifting down to the bottom of the sea. Picture an undisturbed underwater world where nothing is required of you.

JULY 24

Get It All Out

Mind dumps are a great exercise in getting out anything and everything that's taking up space in your head. Set aside fifteen minutes today to cozy up with your journal and dump out everything you can in a stream of consciousness onto a page.

JULY 25

Mindful Chores

When you next need to wash the dishes, set the intention to do so mindfully. Move with purpose, from the moment you turn on the faucet to the moment you turn it off. For every movement that you tend to rush through, do so more deliberately and slowly. Relish the first moment your fingertips touch the water. When you reach for your first dish, feel how your hand stretches, grabs, and holds each one. As you scrub the dishes clean, feel the temperature of the water. Encourage yourself to weave self-care into your daily routine to nourish your empathic abilities—and soul—as you can.

JULY **26**

Trust Your Gut

You may feel weird vibes from certain people who want your attention or empathy. Listen to your gut and remind yourself:

I am free to exit a situation I do not feel safe in.

JULY **27**

Talk to Yourself with Kindness

As a part of self-compassion practice, you can learn how to let go of any judgments and choose to embrace your entire self—flaws, failures, and feelings alike. Reflect on how you talk to yourself—when do you tend to be the most self-critical? Think of three instances of self-talk that are judgmental, pressuring, devaluing, or invalidating and write them down on a big poster. Below each example reflecting self-judgment, write an alternate response rooted in self-kindness. For example: "I should have done more for them" transforms to "I did my best at the time." Say it aloud with confidence as you cross out the self-judgment.

JULY 28

Unaware Empaths

An unaware empath feels easily drained and gets caught up in others' negativity. An intuitive empath can feel others deeply and still maintain an inner balance. Set aside ten minutes to journal about where you see yourself on this spectrum of empathy. Reinforce how far you've come and explore areas in need of growth.

JULY 29

My Inner Knowing

When others question how your emotionality influences your behavior, it's easy to minimize your intuition. Continue to develop trust in your gut because you're usually onto something. Say:

I release doubt and honor my inner knowing.

JULY 30

Research Your Favorite City

Whether or not you're a history buff, this activity will let your emotional self rest while you engage your brain in something fun and informative. Pick a city that interests you—whether you have lived in it before or it's a place you want to visit. Try your luck at finding the oldest photos or maps and reading a bit about the history of the spots you love. Look at the oldest map you can find and compare it to one from the present day. For an extra bit of fun, share your findings with someone who loves the city, too.

JULY 31

Where Does My Empathy Go?

In addition to human emotions and suffering, many empaths care deeply about animals, plants, and the planet. Where else does your empathy extend? What does that look like? Is it more or less difficult to separate yourself from the suffering of nonhuman living things? Take some time to journal about it.

AUGUST 1

Live in Truth

Don't allow anyone to warp your reality:

Say aloud: I trust in my truth. I will not allow someone to influence or manipulate my reality.

AUGUST 2

Inner Child Meditation

Many of your struggles, unmet needs, and old pains can be traced back to events that your younger self experienced. Have you ever spent time to think about what it was like to be an empathic child? If you are able, find a photo of your younger self, sit somewhere quiet, and make yourself comfortable. Look at the photo and really try to connect with the child in the photograph. Bring to mind a vivid image of yourself at an age before twelve. Picture that little self already feeling everything and everyone around them and see if any memories come up of times when you were overcome with a difficult emotion. If and when that happens, allow your attention to settle on a visualization of your current self wrapping your arms around and comforting the little you.

AUGUST 3

Encyclopedia-ing

Self-care doesn't have to be obviously soothing or restorative. It can just be something fun that doesn't tire you
out. Start by searching for a topic you're interested in
online or in an encyclopedia. Read as much as you'd like,
but as soon as your interest is piqued by another topic, go
with it. You may be tempted to read the entire entry, but
instead practice letting it go. There is *infinite* information,
but a *finite* amount of time and energy. Journal about
topics as you go, flagging any that you would like to go
back to at another time. Have fun with where the search
takes you.

AUGUST 4

What Reactions Do I Have?

It's likely that you have emotional reactions to movies,
music, and news. What was the last medium that made
you feel pain or cry? Did this experience further overwhelm you or did it feel cathartic? Are there genres
that are difficult for you to consume? Write about
your experience.

AUGUST 5

You Are Worthy

You deserve the world, dear empath; it's not always about what you can do for it. Remember:

I deserve to express my true needs. I deserve to have my sensitivities respected.

AUGUST 6

Dispel Frustration Meditation

It might be hard to accept, but the reality is that no one's experience of suffering is in your control. You only have control over your response to others—no matter how much you wish to make things different, to fix, to save, to heal. Letting go of control is a powerful way to care for yourself. Sit in a comfortable position. Close your eyes and plant your feet firmly on the ground. Make tight fists. Use your breath to calm and bring your body to the present moment. As you inhale, imagine you are breathing in courage, letting go of anything you're trying to control with your mind. As you exhale, let your hands and fingers uncurl as though you were reeling in a fish with a fishing pole, without fighting the fish to be caught. Repeat to yourself, "I breathe in courage. I breathe out control."

AUGUST 7

Spend Time Alone

Empaths require time to recharge, recalibrate, and enjoy their space. When empaths are alone, they are able to be honest with themselves without absorbing negative energy or anything external steering them off their path. What is your relationship with purposeful alone time? How frequently does it happen? What do you do, and where do you do it? Be honest with yourself in your journal. Then commit to ensuring you reserve the appropriate time needed for *you*.

AUGUST 8

Quiet Loud Feelings

Anytime you're feeling a lot, say to yourself:

I am safe from even the scariest of emotions. They will not harm me.

AUGUST 9

Go Smudging

Smudging is the practice of burning herbs to purify negative energy. When smudging a space, you burn plant material. The smoke fills and purifies the environment. You can use any incense for smudging; however, common go-tos are white sage and palo santo. First, grab your materials. Find some matches and a candle to relight the smudge stick during your activity. Be sure to keep a fireproof container close by. Starting at the entryway, light your smudge stick, and move it in clockwise circles in the air. Walk clockwise around your home or space to smudge, letting smoke fill closed-off spaces, too.

AUGUST 10

How Do I Cope?

It's normal and expected to have some less-healthy coping strategies as you grow into practicing better ones. Write about any unhealthy ways in which you have attempted to deal. How did those coping mechanisms protect you at the time? What protective purpose did they serve?

AUGUST 11

Notice Fear

Fear is the underlying emotion for most of your secondary feelings. For example, you may get sad when someone close to you is going through a rough time. If you look beneath the sadness, you might find a fear of having a loved one suffer while all you can do is stand by and watch. For this practice, feel free to throw a blanket over your lap or shoulders as you drop into your meditative state. A little extra comfort can go a long way. As you bring your focus inward, recall a moment when you've felt afraid. Become aware of how fear turns up in your body. Notice where your mind wanders to when you are fearful. If you have a little extra time, you can add a few minutes of comforting yourself before you end the practice.

AUGUST 12

Holding On to Your Energy

As an empath, you may feel the pull to put your life on hold while you give all your energy to supporting those closest to you. Take ten minutes to journal about aspects of your life where you kept your focus off your plans, goals, and dreams to instead focus on others.

AUGUST 13

Take Up a Hobby

Was there something you enjoyed doing as a child or teen that you don't do much of anymore? Maybe it's writing poetry, playing soccer, photography, or playing video games. Hobbies are amazing outlets for an overflow of emotions. They are opportunities to get out into the world and slow down. Decide to reconnect with the younger *you*. Revive one of your past favorite hobbies and work it into your weekly schedule. Whatever your favorite activity may be, nurturing your hobbies nurtures your heart and allows you to grow and process in your own way.

AUGUST 14

Build Resilience Meditation

To continue as an empath in a chaotic world, you must build up the inner strength that it takes to protect yourself from taking on negative energy. Resilience is self-care. For this thirty-minute practice, stand and face a wall, stretching your arms out directly in front of you until your palms are against it. Close your eyes and begin to bring your attention to the point where your palms meet the wall. Every few breaths, add a bit more force to your arms as if you were needing more and more strength to push the wall away. Notice how your muscles feel as they engage and observe any thoughts or feelings that come up. When your mind wanders, bring your awareness back to the sensation of building strength and envisioning the wall as anything that you want to protect yourself against. Affirm to yourself out loud: "I have the strength to protect myself."

AUGUST 15

Doodling Fun

For your self-care practice today, mix it up—instead of writing, use a journal page to doodle and draw anything that comes to mind. Let go of hesitation and just have a little fun on the page.

AUGUST 16

Trust in Yourself

Your intuition is more often right than it is wrong. Own that with a powerful affirmation:

I am releasing self-doubt and strengthening self-trust.

AUGUST 17

Make a Vision Board

Assemble poster board, scissors, glue, and a magazine collection. Then set aside thirty minutes for this activity. Pick an aspect of your life that could use a dash of inspiration or motivation. Have you been wanting to start your own business, redecorate your space, or work on an area of self-growth? Flip through the magazines and clip out anything that has relatable content. Cut out words and images that support or align with your vision and paste them to a poster. When you have completed your board of inspiration, display it somewhere prominent that will help motivate you.

AUGUST 18

Hypervigilance Alleviation Meditation

Overcoming hypervigilance is a common issue for empaths. Arriving with your whole self in the present moment, remind yourself that there is nowhere else to be right now but here. Give yourself the time you deserve to slow down and regulate your nervous system. As you follow the sound of your breath, tell yourself that you are safe to relax your mind and body. Visualize a vivid image of a sunset and imagine you can see every detail of the color patterns in the sky and on the water. Notice how the image becomes softer as the sun slowly disappears below the horizon, and everything around you is less in focus. Hold in mind the softened scene, remembering that it is safe to let go of paying such close attention in your daily life.

AUGUST 19

Words to Self-Soothe

It's important to have some soothing self-talk in your back pocket during moments of high tension or energy. Affirm:

My anxiety is not based on reality. I perceive the world with love.

AUGUST 20

Creature Therapy

Hanging out with creatures of the furry—or scaly—variety helps put life into perspective. Creatures don't have egos and inherently live a more mindful existence, which is something humans could benefit from learning. Find a local animal shelter to pet some dogs, go to a nearby farm to feed the horses, or offer to babysit your friend's new kitten. Whatever you do, go slightly out of the way to spend some quality time with an animal friend. Enjoy an interaction free of emotional upheaval and bask in the simplicity of being alongside an amazing living creature.

AUGUST 21

Mindful Movement Meditation

Find a spot where you have plenty of space in front of and around you with little distractions. Set a timer for ten minutes. With a soft gaze focused on the ground before you, choose a part of your body where you can observe movement. Bring yourself into the present moment by feeling the way this body part can be manipulated. Observe both its range and its restrictions—be mindful of where movement becomes discomfort. Focus your attention on any muscles, joints, bones, or skin that participate in the motion. Spend some time visualizing what the anatomy looks like on the inside. Can you picture the muscle as it tenses and relaxes? Imagine how the bones and joints in the area interact to create movement. Feel free at any time to shift to another part of your body during the meditation and follow the same steps of observation.

AUGUST 22

Stay Appreciative

Find a quiet space, pull out your journal, and take five minutes to pen a letter of gratitude to yourself for wherever you are on your self-growth self-care journey. Be kind and supportive to you!

AUGUST 23

Practice Acceptance

You may experience discomfort from wanting so badly to help, heal, or fix, and from continuing to try, despite an inability to do so. Say:

I accept that I cannot help everyone. I accept that I cannot heal anyone.

AUGUST 24

Float Away Meditation

Taking good care of yourself includes knowing how to bring a sense of levity anytime you're feeling the weight of the world on your shoulders. Find a quiet space and sit comfortably, letting a chair or wall support your back so that you don't have to use much energy to hold yourself up. As you take in your first breath, imagine that you are a deflated balloon. Each breath of air fills you up more and more until you become aware of lightness in your body. You notice that every part of you is weightless as you float off the floor, nothing tethering you to the ground. When thinking takes over, bring your mind back to the feeling of effortlessness and weightlessness. Spend ten minutes envisioning yourself floating peacefully over cities, occasionally getting caught in the clouds. Repeat to yourself, "I am weightless."

AUGUST 25

Wildlife Entertainment

National Geographic is popular for showcasing bonds between humans and animals, as well as the natural habitats and behaviors of the earth's creatures. Whether it's watching TV or flipping through a magazine, use reality entertainment to connect with wildlife you may not otherwise see. Enjoy learning about creatures that have entirely different worlds and demand nothing of humans. Observe and marvel in the simplicity of animal behavior. Be sure to put any devices away so you can engross yourself in this experience. Tip: Steer clear of shows or articles that feature climate change or animal harm, as those issues can heavily trigger empaths.

AUGUST 26

Overwhelming Confrontations

Sometimes being *you* can feel like a blessing—and a curse. Have you ever encountered someone who tried to talk to you about being too much? Take some journal time to explore what that situation brought up inside you. How have you healed? Is that person still in your life?

AUGUST 27

Seek Reiki

Reiki is a meditative practice rooted in ancient Chinese and Japanese medicine. It reduces stress and anxiety and promotes relaxation. Empaths can use Reiki's specific techniques to clear and purify built-up energy. A common Reiki technique to perform on yourself is called "hands to the head." Resting your palms on your skull, cup your head, and let your fingertips touch at the very top. Focus your attention on your hands. Allow this position to relax the muscles and skin on your head. Do this for two minutes. Alternatively, you can search online to find a local practitioner who can provide you with expert guidance and therapy in person.

AUGUST 28

Live in Detachment

Today, there is no preamble necessary. Just say this on repeat:

I am able to observe my emotions without becoming attached to them.

AUGUST **29**

Tranquility Stretch Meditation

In this practice, you will get into some deep stretches as you rest your awareness on the slow, intentional movement of your body. Sit up straight or stand tall, feeling free to close your eyes or keep them open if that is more comfortable. On the in-breath, lengthen your spine as you're able; on the slow out-breath, bring your chin to your chest and begin to roll down. Focus your attention on each vertebra as you continue to bend. Feel your palms against your thighs and knees as they slide down with you. Feel the bend in your knees. When you've reached a place where you cannot roll down any farther, stretch down another inch on the out-breath. Let your head hang as you let go of any tension. On your way back up, straighten your spine as you're able to, mindfully, bit by bit. Bring the tranquility of the moment up with you as you sit or stand up tall.

AUGUST **30**

Stay Balanced

Being pulled in so many directions makes it difficult to live a balanced life at times. Take ten minutes to journal about what you have done in the last few days to cultivate a greater sense of inner peace and calm. Be sure to journal about what has gotten in your way.

AUGUST 31

Your ego is what tells you that you need to keep meeting others' expectations of you. Set your intention:

I choose to ignore my ego and to listen to my higher self instead.

SEPTEMBER 1

Refresh Your Bedroom

Engaging in self-care is also choosing to take care of an outstanding chore or errand that will ultimately bring more comfort or ease to your life. When was the last time you changed your sheets, covers, and pillowcases? Washed your towels? Bought some fresh flowers for a lonely vase? Choose five elements of your bedroom that could use a refresh. Try not to get into a cleaning frenzy unless that genuinely de-stresses you. Otherwise, focus on the sensation of bringing in clean, new energy into your resting space.

SEPTEMBER 2

What Would I Turn Off?

If you could have an on-and-off switch for your abilities (e.g., emotional attunement, noticing tiny changes in
behavior, being the friend group's therapist), what would
you do when your switch was off? Set aside ten minutes
to journal about your thoughts.

SEPTEMBER 3

Light amid Darkness

Have you ever absorbed the suffering from your
surrounding environment and felt hopeless and bleak?
Affirm the opposite of how you feel:

*I focus my energy on all the joy and positivity that exists
in the world.*

SEPTEMBER 4

Return to Peace Meditation

It's helpful to keep a few memories in your back pocket of moments where you felt particularly content and tranquil. They are great ways to shift your attention to a more relaxing object of focus. Lie on your back with your legs and arms splayed out to the sides. As you close your eyes, feel the weight of your body being held up by the floor. Pick a memory that evokes a sense of peace and serenity and visualize it in as much detail as you can recall. Observe what happens in your body as you imagine what it felt like to experience a deep sense of calm. Do your limbs relax? Does a smile paint across your face? Anytime you get distracted, reorient yourself by saying: "I am returning to the peaceful place."

SEPTEMBER 5

Sleep Maintenance

For those nights when you're up late and can't sleep, choose to grab your notebook instead. Take a deep breath in and breathe out slowly. Write about what's keeping you up. What comforting words can you say to yourself to help you fall asleep?

SEPTEMBER 6

I Give Myself Time

Don't fret if you struggle with putting up mental protection—it's a process that will take time. Slow things down by saying:

I am learning how to set healthier boundaries.

SEPTEMBER 7

Wear a Long-Lost Item

There's always an item hanging at the back of the closet or smooshed in an ancient pile of clothes yearning to be worn. You don't have to be a fashionista to forget about a shirt you bought but never wore. It can feel empowering to put together a new outfit combination highlighting the gently worn piece. Try to push yourself outside of your comfort zone by finding enjoyment in the playfulness of this activity. Whether you choose to wear the outfit to an occasion or throw yourself a fashion show, don't take yourself too seriously—that's what self-care is all about.

SEPTEMBER 8

Cut the Cord Meditation

You can learn to let go of old stagnant stories, emotions, and energy to make room for healthy, loving, and expansive experiences that serve your highest self. Get into a comfortable seated position and set your timer for ten minutes. Focus your attention on the initial deep breaths, letting your lungs and belly expand. Begin to imagine that there are cords tied around you and each one is attached to a different thing that holds you back or harms you. Visualize how the weight of all the cords is pulling at your body and dragging you down. With each set of breaths, focus on just one cord and see vividly what it is tied to. Imagine you can take a scissor and cut the cord, one stressor at a time. With each cut, fill your lungs and belly with air and breathe out as you sever each attachment.

SEPTEMBER 9

Reflect on Self-Growth

Someday soon, your self-care practice will be much more reflexive and intuitive. What might look different one year from now if you really incorporate all the different things in this book into your routine? Write about how your practices will contribute to your self-growth.

SEPTEMBER 10

I Am the Architect of My Life

Recall something that you have said you couldn't do that is feasible with a little more patience and practice. Say:

I am the architect of my life. I choose what I want it to look like.

SEPTEMBER 11

Heal in the Outdoors

Taking refuge in the earth's natural landscapes speeds up an empath's recovery from all the stress, worry, and suffering they absorb. Take an opportunity to connect with the outdoors in an accessible way. Try going fishing, taking a hike, or going on a train ride through the countryside. Notice the scenery, weather, and fragrances. If you can't adventure elsewhere, try sunset sky-gazing. Grab a chair or lie in the grass and look up. Notice what you see, saying it aloud to remain in the present moment, whether it's the color-changing sky or any other natural phenomenon that you observe.

SEPTEMBER 12

Healing Hands Meditation

When you offer yourself a comforting touch or squeeze, your body's care system is activated. This care system downregulates your fight-or-flight response and helps you ground yourself with physical touch. Sit up so that you have access to all parts of your body. You can stretch your legs out in front of you or cross them if you'd like. As you begin your usual deep-breathing routine, start to scan your body for stress, anxiety, discomfort, or pain. When you locate an area like your tight chest, for instance, guide your palm and place it comfortably over your heart space. As you breathe in and out, imagine you are sending healing energy through your palms. Feel the warmth of skin against skin as you move your hand to various parts of your body and apply a loving pressure, sending signals of safety to your brain.

SEPTEMBER 13

Relish in the World's Beauty

For every bit of suffering that the world encounters, bliss, awe, and wonder is felt, too. Remember the magic that surrounds us by affirming:

I am enchanted with life.

SEPTEMBER 14

My Favorite Affirmation

Reflecting on the affirmations you have come across in this book and elsewhere, write about one that is meaningful yet difficult to practice. At the end of your thoughts, write that affirmation ten times over, being intentional each time you repeat it to yourself.

SEPTEMBER 15

I Am Unique

When it gets frustrating to hold space for everyone and everything, bring this statement to mind:

I am unique in this way. It is okay that others are different from me.

SEPTEMBER 16

Find Something Special

Most empaths like a space where their energy is protected, rather than drained further. No matter the
aesthetic (or lack thereof), everyone enjoys having special
objects or touches in their space—trinkets that remind
you of a trip you took or a cool, vintage lamp you finally
pulled the trigger on. The intention is to do something that
specifically benefits you and *your* wants and needs. Go
out on a little adventure and find one thing to add to your
home that brings you a sense of calm and delight. Every
time you encounter your new object, remember that it is a
source for grounding.

SEPTEMBER 17

Fall Reflections

You've gotten though a large portion of this book by now.
Take ten to fifteen minutes to reflect on and journal about
how your self-care intentions and implementation have
transformed over that time. What's one behavior you
would still like to change or incorporate?

SEPTEMBER 18

The Eye of the Storm

When a conversation comes head-to-head, or a moment becomes too intense, affirm the following:

I send this intensity back to its creator with love. I live in peace and calm.

SEPTEMBER 19

Do a Fun Grocery Run

Trying to efficiently navigate crowds means you've likely learned how to get in and get out of the grocery store instead of roaming the aisles. For your next grocery trip for nonessentials, give yourself a budget and imagine you're going on a field trip. Go into your favorite supermarket as though it were your first time. Wander down each aisle, examining products you've never looked at before. Put together a small basket of treats, like a delicious cheese and a set of crackers, or granola and a Greek yogurt with an intriguing flavor. Pretend you are your younger self picking yummy snacks off the shelves.

SEPTEMBER 20

Keep a Full Tank

It is easy to run on empty for too long before you realize you burned out three conversations ago. Remind yourself of this regularly:

Just because I can do it, doesn't mean I always should.

SEPTEMBER 21

Human Connection Meditation

The deeper your understanding of the shared human existence, the easier it will be for you to find harmony within yourself in relation to the rest of the world. Feel your feet pressing down against the floor as you begin to observe your mind. Recall any challenging thoughts that come up regularly. Do you notice any themes of worry, belonging, or self-criticism? As your breath travels through your body, think of a person who has struggled with a similar pattern of thinking—someone who regularly commiserates with or validates you. Visualize the two of you holding hands and standing side by side. With each breath, add a new person to the chain. Imagine five people from every country joining to link hands. Even at minimum, over six hundred people stand side by side who have experienced similar struggles. Meditate on the notion that you are not alone.

SEPTEMBER 22

My Experiences Are My Own

Comparing and contrasting two opposing experiences can highlight what you still need to work on when it comes to setting boundaries. Journal about one instance in the last week where you didn't protect your spirit. Follow this up by reflecting on a recent time when you did. What did you do differently between the two experiences?

SEPTEMBER 23

I Am Resilient

When emotions are getting the better of you and you're finding it difficult to maintain your calm, it's helpful to channel the resilient earth. Affirm:

I am rooted like a tree. I am steady like a mountain.

SEPTEMBER 24

Watch a Classic Movie

Who could resist the recommendation to practice self-care by watching a beloved, favorite movie? Everyone has those days when it feels impossible to settle on what to watch. With seemingly endless streaming services, the choices are genuinely overwhelming. Whether you're feeling burnt out from your day or you just want to kick back, you may not want to pay attention to anything that requires focus and cognitive processing. So when complex character and plot development is not the right vibe, reach for a lighthearted go-to of your era. Pick a film that will let you enjoy rather than engage.

SEPTEMBER 25

Emotional Health Maintenance

Set aside ten minutes to reflect on and complete the following sentences within your journal:

I will continue to take care of my emotional health by:

I will continue to take care of my body by:

I will continue to set my intentions to:

I will choose myself because:

SEPTEMBER 26

Resist Judgment

When others are committed to misunderstanding you, protect yourself by stating:

I am unaffected by the judgment of others. I witness situations without judgment.

SEPTEMBER 27

Seek Out Water

Lakes, rivers, streams, ponds, reservoirs, oceans, canals—whichever body of water is calling your name, head to it. If swimming or dipping your feet is an option, even better. When you arrive, find a spot where you can comfortably post up for at least thirty minutes. Leave your phone out of it—this is your opportunity to let any stresses wash away with the burbling of the water before you. Go on a little hunt for seashells or flat rocks you can skip against the surface—there's nothing else needing your attention in this moment.

SEPTEMBER 28

A Meditation to Unwind

What kind of mental imagery does the word "unwind" bring up for you? Breathe in deeply through the nose and breathe out slowly through pursed lips. Notice how your body is feeling, noting any tightness or tension in the present moment. Begin to visualize what it would look and feel like to pull at the end of twine wrapped tightly around your body. Envision that with each round of unwinding, more stress dissipates. For a more tangible object meditation, grab a piece of string and repeat the process of twirling it around your finger and then unwinding it. Pay attention to the sensation of tightness, followed by the sensation of loosening the string and feeling the blood rushing back to your finger. Imagine that you could feel just as free from any emotional or relational burdens. On the inhale, visualize the sensations of binding; on the exhale, unravel yourself into relaxation.

SEPTEMBER 29

Go at a Snail's Pace

Practice the art of choosing to slow yourself down or to take a break by gently reassuring yourself:

I've done enough. It's okay to stop for now.

SEPTEMBER **30**

What Do My Negative Thoughts Say?

Check-in time! Set aside ten minutes, pull out your journal, and find somewhere quiet. What are the negative thoughts that you need to free from your mind today? List them. Then release them through writing. Start each sentence with: "I release . . ."

OCTOBER I

Affirm Your Need to Rest

Every empath could use a catchy mantra to throw around whenever they need a reminder to pause and practice. Here's one for you to try:

Rest to restore, rest to replenish, rest to renew.

OCTOBER 2

Experiment with an Acupressure Mat

You can enhance some self-care practices with items designed specifically for stress alleviation. If you don't already have one, order an acupressure mat ASAP. It has mini plastic spikes that stimulate blood flow in whatever part of the body you press against it. Increased blood flow to muscles encourages them to relax. When you have fifteen minutes to spend undisturbed, lay your bare back against the mat. Feel the heat emanating from your back and shift your weight around to see how the pressure feels in varying positions. Alternatively, you can also stand on the mat with bare feet and engage in a mindfulness practice.

OCTOBER 3

Blue Sky Meditation

When emotions overtake you, they blind you to what's underneath all the turmoil: the *you* who is inherently mindful. Lie down in a comfortable position and draw your attention inward. Close your eyes and imagine a bright blue sky. Like the mind, the sky is a blank canvas on which thoughts, emotions, and experiences appear. Imagine that a cloud rolls in, and another, and another, until the sky is gray with no sunrays to be found. Some turn into thunderstorms. Observe your fixation on the clouds (thoughts, feelings, events). Zoom out and bring your awareness to the entire scene so you can see the clouds and the sky up above, like layers on a cake.

OCTOBER 4

Tell Your Tale

Have you ever given an elevator pitch about yourself for a class or during an interview? Imagine you are trying to influence fellow empaths to get excited about self-care. Give a three-minute roundup of your experience as a highly sensitive empath going through the exercises in this book.

OCTOBER 5

Shield of Light

The next time someone, or something, starts to cross a boundary, imagine you are inside a bright orb of light and state:

My inner balance is always protected by this shield made of light.

OCTOBER 6

Give Back

Giving back is a wonderful way to fulfill your desire to help others in a way that feels empowering. When you volunteer, there is a communal feeling that is undeniably moving and you can leave knowing that you've contributed in a meaningful way. Search for volunteer opportunities in your area and choose a gig that reflects your core values and gets you excited to help. You can post up in a kitchen, call bingo at a senior center, or teach neurodivergent students reading skills at the local library. Log how you feel before, during, and after the shift to track any patterns relevant to your self-care.

OCTOBER 7

Lessons from the Past

Empaths not only feel others deeply but are also often excellent readers of the nuances of human behavior. However, sometimes your emotional state can cloud your intuition. Journal about a recent experience when you didn't trust your instincts, and it negatively impacted you and/or the situation at hand.

OCTOBER 8

Protect Your Energy

During your life, have you noticed that you seem to attract people who require a lot of your energy? You're not the only one! As you begin your day, say aloud:

I attract only those with whom I align.

OCTOBER 9

Dance Wildly

Dancing is a form of movement that gives you a guaranteed happiness boost—moving your body to music or sound is an act that goes back to ancient times. Dance sets free any stagnant or negative energy. Find a time during the day when you can put on some music and begin to dance in whatever way your body naturally wants to move. If you catch yourself holding back, remind yourself of the freeing nature of letting loose and moving rhythmically. As you dance, offer yourself the following affirmation: "I care about you very much and you deserve to feel unrestrained and unburdened."

OCTOBER 10

Do I Hold Back the Truth?

Many empaths will hold back from telling the whole truth to protect someone else from experiencing discomfort—sometimes at their own expense. Today, take ten to fifteen minutes to let it off your chest by reflecting and journaling. What are you keeping to yourself?

OCTOBER 11

Count on Support

You don't have to go through difficult times on your own, even though it may feel uncomfortable to look for support. Affirm:

I am allowed to ask for help.

OCTOBER 12

Rain over Resistance Meditation

Turn on the sound of rain hitting a body of water and sit cross-legged on the floor or on a cushion. Bring your focus to the sound of the rain as it hits the surface. When you catch yourself thinking, become aware of how each thought is like a raindrop. When it hits, it creates ripples—during a hard rain (an influx of thoughts), the many ripples make it difficult to see beneath the surface (insight). Trying to dive in to see the bottom will create more waves, and you'll find yourself in murky waters. Visualize the patience that it takes to wait for the rain to stop and for the water to become still again.

OCTOBER 13

Live in Balance

Regularly reflecting on the qualities of those you admire is a great way to channel your energy. In your journal, list a few people you don't know in real life whom you feel represent a great balance between sensitivity and confidence (e.g., authors, celebrities, people you follow on social media). Write about what you can take and practice from these empathic role models.

OCTOBER 14

Can I Let Go?

What will you practice letting go of today? What will take its place? Say:

I am releasing comparison to gain an appreciation of all that I am.

OCTOBER 15

Bake a Sweet Treat

If your greatest baking achievement was putting drops of raw cookie dough onto a pan, not to worry. Only choose something complicated if you're up for it, but focus on picking a recipe you'll enjoy the process of following. Baking is precise and therefore easily lends itself as an opportunity to practice a mindful approach. When you catch yourself rushing through a step or getting antsy, take a deep breath in and remind yourself that you're just having fun taking a break from anything energy-zapping. Practice patience and enjoy your baked treat! If it feels more pleasant, enlist the help of a calming friend to bake alongside you.

OCTOBER 16

When It's Not Reciprocated

You are a natural at understanding others. Unfortunately, that doesn't always get reciprocated. How do you react when you feel misunderstood? Take some time to reflect. Then, journal about any fears that hold you back from communicating your emotional needs in relationships—work, familial, and personal.

OCTOBER 17

Rescuing Others, or Not

You can't save anyone from themselves, even with your superpowers. It sucks, but it's powerful to accept that truth. Say:

It is not in my power to rescue anyone and that is okay.

OCTOBER 18

Try Yoga

Carve out thirty minutes to learn and to practice three yoga poses. For example, spend five minutes or so settling into each of the following three poses: mountain, downward-facing dog, and cat/cow alternation. Stay in each pose thirty seconds longer than you feel you can, mindfully noting any restlessness that may arise. Remember that you are taking care of your body, which is ultimately the vessel for all the listening, understanding, and validating that you do. If you are familiar with all the poses, pick three to focus your attention on that you would like to deepen your practice in.

OCTOBER 19

Release Effort Meditation

Have you ever gotten ready for bed, gotten comfortable, but couldn't fall asleep? The harder you tried, the more difficult it became to sleep? Turns out that sleep cannot be forced. It is only when you stop trying that you let go and drift off. In your meditation today, observe the reflex to try to get yourself to stop thinking. Notice when you're striving for a particular outcome when all you're meant to do is to breathe and watch the inner workings of your mind. Now imagine that your mind is like a wandering puppy. If you put it in its crate, it will cry until you set it free again. Instead of having to constantly get up and chase the puppy to bring it back, visualize having a long rope with lots of slack that can keep the puppy safe while it explores.

OCTOBER **20**

How Do My Childhood Experiences Shape Me?

There are moments of childhood that reflect your most uninhibited nature, free of the burdens of your own emotional stress and that of others. Pull out your journal, get comfortable, and write about what you most enjoyed doing as a child. Come up with some ideas about how to incorporate your childlike self into your self-care.

OCTOBER **21**

Manifest Calm

Reaffirming your desire to manifest a calm and steady nature an extra time won't hurt:

I am filled with peaceful energy and stillness.

OCTOBER 22

Acts of Service

Empaths primarily think of and do things for others, but self-care means practicing turning off the empath auto-pilot to explore human connection without attachment. Engaging in low-effort gestures of kindness helps refill your emotional gas tank. Choose a day when you will have the opportunity to encounter a variety of people and places. Maybe you're planning to ride local transportation or work at a coffee shop. Try offering up your seat, paying for someone's coffee, or contributing to a donations jar. See what moves you toward a kind gesture. Delight in how restorative it feels.

OCTOBER 23

Soothe Burnout Meditation

You're likely very familiar with the experience of burning out. Neglecting self-care when you're in a constant state of energy absorption and depletion is a fast track to paralyzing exhaustion. Whether you're approaching the tipping point or have already entered the throes of burnout, this is a chance for you to alleviate all that you have been carrying around with you. With a yoga mat or rug underneath you, come down on all fours and mindfully transition into child's pose. As you breathe in through the nose, walk your fingertips away from you and feel a deep stretch of the spine. Breathe out slowly through your mouth as you push your hips back a little farther into your seat. Every few minutes, sink farther into the elongated posture and embrace the restfulness of spending time in this position.

OCTOBER **24**

Devote Time to Goals

A lot of empaths sacrifice giving attention to what they want because so much of their time and energy goes to others. It often goes unnoticed if you are someone who chronically minimizes the importance of your own experience. In your journal, list five daydreams, interests, or goals that are important to you. Reflect on how much of your time you give to each of these.

OCTOBER **25**

Allow It to Pass

Negative emotions can feel too intense when you forget that they are temporary. Affirm:

This emotion is just a visitor passing through. It means no harm.

OCTOBER 26

Visit a Dog Park

Even if you're a cat person, sitting in a park and watching dogs be dogs is objectively amusing. Getting to see animals outside connects you with nature in a profound way. Find a bench in a dog park or a dog-filled park. Spend thirty minutes mindfully observing how dogs walk, run, and behave. If you see two dogs interacting, come up with voices for each dog and pretend they're having a conversation. Silliness is your self-care today!

OCTOBER 27

Ride the Wave Meditation

If you were swimming in the ocean, what would happen if you began to swim against the current? Not only would you get exhausted quickly, but you also wouldn't get very far. When your sea gets rough, close your eyes, and feel your body sink into its seat. Note any emotional turbulence and pay attention to its rise and fall, seeing how feelings mimic the ocean waves. Sometimes the wave crashes over your head and you're knocked around below the surface, coming up gasping for air. Imagine, however, that you have the option of surfing your emotional waves. Instead of getting caught up in a difficult emotion, visualize yourself skimming just the surface of the experience. Continue to maintain your focus on noting what kind of emotions are coming up, but not letting them overtake you.

OCTOBER 28

I Am Light

When you're feeling stressed or overwhelmed from emotional labor, use this mantra:

I am light. I am peace. I am balance. Repeat.

OCTOBER 29

Savor Delightful Tastes

Think of a restaurant you haven't been to in a while, or a recipe that you enjoy but takes forever to make. Make a reservation or pick up the ingredients you need to reconnect with your favorite flavor experience. As you sit down in the restaurant, or as you start to cook, recall the enjoyment you experienced the last time you were here. What about this experience, or food, delighted your mind? What did the food taste like? What does it bring up for you? Reconnecting with your inner bliss is an effective way to negate the emotion and harshness of the world.

OCTOBER 30

What Are My Needs? Meditation

Many empaths forget about their own needs in order
to prioritize those of others. Once you've acknowledged
yourself as being a chronic self-neglecter, the next step is
to identify your needs in various settings and relationships.
Thanks to heightened intuition, you probably know a lot
about what those are—you just haven't always advocated
for yourself. Choose one need at a time, one per meditation. Find a spot that can support your back and close your
eyes. Start by asking yourself, "What is a priority need of
mine?" Focus on a need that is present that day or in that
exact moment—it can be as simple as needing hydration.
Notice any discomfort that may arise when acknowledging
or requesting something that you require for your overall
well-being. Visualize yourself vocalizing this need without
apology and picture having it successfully met.

OCTOBER 31

I Am Proud

Not only is self-care important, but so too is self-praise.
Take notice of all the work you've done up to this point.
Congratulate yourself! Affirm:

I am proud of my growth, gosh dang it!

NOVEMBER 1

Go to a Museum

Choose a museum to visit that is small to medium in size, or pick a collection or two to explore in a larger museum. Adventure by yourself to lock in some alone time, too. Whatever type of destination you pick, be sure that its contents don't bring you more stress. The natural history museum in any city is a great example of a place you can roam around in for a couple of hours, learn some fun facts, feel like a kid again, and not come home feeling like you missed out because you couldn't get close enough to the *Mona Lisa* to take a selfie.

NOVEMBER 2

The Effect of Others

The people whom you surround yourself with have a significant impact on your mental health. Set aside time to write: list three to five people you spend the majority of your time with. Explore all the facets of how each affect your emotions, thoughts, and behaviors. Are there any changes you want to make that would benefit your emotional wellness?

NOVEMBER 3

I Have a Community

If you ever feel like an outsider, reaffirm your belonging:

I trust that I belong in a loving community, even when it doesn't feel like it.

NOVEMBER 4

Count to Ten

Shift your energy away from your emotional center over to fun, no-pressure, mental stimulation. Is there a language you've always wanted to learn? Or a language that you *never* thought you'd want to become fluent in? Choose one—like Italian, French, or Turkish—and learn how to count to ten. Pull up a language app or listen to a local to get the most accurate pronunciation. Once memorized, record a voice note and play it back to yourself to see where you can use a little more practice. For an extra challenge, watch a foreign film in that language. When your mind is focused on processing subtitles and new sounds, it won't have many cognitive resources left for wandering to topics that cause frustration, upset, or exhaustion. As a bonus, you'll now be able to count to ten in a new language!

NOVEMBER 5

Stay Retrospective

As the end of the year approaches, break the year down into four seasons and journal about where you were at regarding your self-awareness and self-care during winter, spring, summer, and autumn. Use the seasons as markers of change, making it easier to recall and write down what changes you observed within yourself.

NOVEMBER 6

Beware of Over-Apologizing

Apologizing too frequently is often indicative of minimizing yourself and your experience. So what to do? Affirm:

I feel confident in my every word, deed, and step forward.

NOVEMBER 7

Get It Out

It's time to be you, dear empath, and that means being honest with yourself about things you may otherwise bury, like the qualities of individuals who set off your annoyance bells. Take ten minutes to let yourself journal about the people and their qualities that upset you sometimes. Let it flow!

NOVEMBER 8

Surrender to Uncertainty

Life is filled with uncertainty, but humans will do anything to minimize the discomfort of not knowing what's to come. The best you can do is learn to surrender yourself to it because there is no chance of making uncertainty go away. Find a quiet place and sit comfortably. As you settle into your upright posture, feel the ground beneath your seat and the weight of your body against it. Take a few deep breaths to orient yourself to the present moment, beginning to draw your shoulders back to stretch open your chest and rib cage area. Alongside the movement, call to mind the following phrases: "I surrender to uncertainty. Uncertainty is nothing to fear." Pay special attention to your mind's attempts to start thinking about something unknown in the future and bring yourself back by repeating the words.

NOVEMBER 9

Take a New Path

Choose your preferred, safe, and typical physical method of moving around during your day. Consciously moving around is a wonderful way of taking care of your mental health because it's an inherently peaceful activity where you can slow down and get distracted by pleasant things around you. You can travel as near or far as you'd like. Whether it's just outside of your home or indoors, set your intention on finding a new path. Turn left when you'd usually turn right. Instead of going from the bed straight to the bathroom, move to the yoga mat instead. Give yourself plenty of time to practice being curious about everything around you.

NOVEMBER 10

I Forgive Myself

Self-care for an empath means a daily dose of self-forgiveness. Say aloud:

I forgive myself for anything I'm hard on myself for.

NOVEMBER 11

What Have I Declined?

If you're this far in this book, hopefully you've had a little practice saying no and setting a few helpful boundaries that protect your feeling-filled soul. Now, make a list of everything you've said no to alongside everything you'd like to say no to. What goals can you set for yourself as you move forward in your empath life?

NOVEMBER 12

I Will Show Myself Kindness

You're forgiving of other people's flaws, but you may not always offer yourself the same kindness. Say:

I am flawed and that makes me human. I am imperfect and that makes me unique.

NOVEMBER 13

Express Gratitude

When you practice gratitude, your brain ceases to be anxious or stressed—even if only for a few moments. Making gratitude a habit is even more effective to reduce any suffering that you experience due to your empathic ways. Choose three people in your life whom you feel thankful for/toward. Write down a statement expressing your gratitude for each person on separate pieces of paper, and send some snail mail to each of those people if you can. Imagine what it will feel like for them to open such an unexpected and loving note.

NOVEMBER 14

Time to Get Cold Meditation

The ability to regulate your nervous system when it's overactive is a skill that takes a lot of practice and focus. This meditation will focus on cultivating the feeling of various sensations. If you're able, refrain from being bundled up or wearing long sleeves or pants. If you can, sit near an open window or outside on a cool night. As you bring your awareness inside your body, let go of any sounds that you may hear. Begin to turn your attention to the feeling of being cold. What does that feel like? Imagine the icy winter wind or walking barefoot on a glacier. Visualize what it would feel like if the chill went down to your bones. In time, you may notice that you shiver just at the thought.

NOVEMBER 15

Journaling Expressions

Sometimes you may feel pressured to journal, as though you have to fill up the pages with painful things; but that's not the case. There doesn't have to be anything that is wrong or unsatisfactory in order for you to journal your thoughts. Journaling is simply writing down your thoughts and feelings to understand them more clearly. Practice this notion by describing some mundane details of your day without opinions or embellishments. Capture your everyday thoughts.

NOVEMBER 16

Welcome Change

The next time your self-growth feels stagnant, or you lose a habit you were building, remind yourself:

I am always in the process of change.

NOVEMBER 17

Record Thoughts of the Day

Logging your thoughts each day is a great way to uncover thinking patterns that make it more difficult to be you. Grab a notebook and start by getting any present thoughts onto the paper. Every few hours, or at least two or three times a day, check in and unload the contents of your mind. At the end of a week, acknowledge any negative patterns, such as catastrophizing or all-or-nothing thinking. Do you ruminate most during a particular time of the day or around certain people? Go the extra mile, jot down more details about each set of thoughts, such as precipitating events or consequences of said thinking.

NOVEMBER 18

A Beginner's Mind Meditation

As you've learned, curiosity is a state of awareness that combats judgment and biases. Being curious is also an effective way to diminish a fearful state. You can approach any familiar thing as though you were doing it for the first time. Pick up virtually any handheld object and place it somewhere at eye level a foot or so in front of you. Focus your attention on the object before you. Imagine you have never heard of it before, so you move with caution and question what the object is, looking at it from every angle, noticing its shape and texture. Next, slowly pick up the object and feel it in your hands. Touch it with your eyes open and closed, bringing it up against your skin and under your nose.

NOVEMBER 19

Retreat into Nature

Finding a peaceful retreat in nature is something that many empaths benefit greatly from. Journal about the last immersive experience you had in nature. What did nature provide you with that is difficult to get elsewhere?

NOVEMBER 20

Write a Note

Complete the following activity as though you were doing it for a best friend. On ten scraps of paper, write down five affirmations and five empowering practices that address the challenges of being an empath. The notes could say "You are really powerful and funny" and "You are going to successfully set boundaries with your family members." Once you've written ten notes, ask someone to hide them inside various nooks and crannies in your home, like in between books on a shelf or tucked in the leaves of a plant. Over time, you will stumble upon these notes and get to feel uplifted by their messages.

NOVEMBER 21

I Deserve Something Special

You've probably spent money to help someone out or gifted a loved one something pricey that you haven't gifted yourself. Affirm that you're worth a little splurge:

I deserve to spend money on something special for myself.

NOVEMBER 22

Practice Relying on Others

Calling attention to yourself by asking for help may feel uncomfortable, but it's important to practice what you preach. Take five to ten minutes to list any issues that could use outside support. Perhaps you're hosting a dinner party and instead of cooking all the dishes, you ask a close friend to whip up a recipe or two to lighten your load. Or maybe you've been too fearful of burdening someone with your recent frustrations with your partner. Now would be your chance to reach out to someone nonjudgmental to whom you could vent about it. Choose two issues of varying urgency from the list to ask for support on.

NOVEMBER 23

Mountaintop Meditation

Sitting on the floor or couch, cross your legs and take a deep, soulful breath in. On your out-breath, visualize yourself comfortable and safe atop a mountain. Picture how quiet it is, feeling the warmth of the blazing sun and the cold of the snow beneath you. Become aware of the strength and stability of the mountain beneath you. It is immovable and impenetrable, providing a sense of stability nothing else can offer. Even when the weather gets rough, imagine that you are always found just above it, unaffected. Take in a deep breath, gathering all the empowering energy provided to you by the mountain. You are merely an observer; there is nothing to do but to see. Carry this energy with you daily and you will experience a greater strength in withstanding the tumults of being an empath.

NOVEMBER 24

My Authentic Self

You haven't always been the kindest or most accepting of aspects of your authentic self. You owe yourself a genuine apology:

I am so sorry for every time I devalued you.

NOVEMBER 25

Write a Travel Wish List

Getting out of an emotional state and getting creative is a brilliant way to create a much-needed shift of energy. Grab paper or poster board and get online to print out inspiring photos from various places you want to go. On one sheet of paper, glue some beautiful scenes onto the page and jot down everything you would like to do when you go there. Have as much fun finding unique pictures of experiences as you did on your vision board. Let your mind daydream about being in the desired location and feeling joyful and fulfilled. Put the finished product somewhere you can frequently glance at for inspiration.

NOVEMBER 26

Reach Beyond Feelings

To strengthen your emotional intelligence, you learn to see beyond feelings to the reasons for them. When you practice understanding and explaining the cause behind an emotion, it helps you see things more broadly. Use your journal to explore three emotions you frequently experience and reflect on what scenarios tend to bring those feelings to the forefront.

NOVEMBER 27

I Release People-Pleasing Behavior

Celebrate the end of people-pleasing behavior by affirming:

I don't have to adapt to the energy in the room. I can influence the energy in the room.

NOVEMBER 28

Watch the Clouds

It's time to watch the clouds roll by! You can stare out a big window or lie back on a blanket on a grassy knoll, taking in everything the sky has to offer. Imagine that you could put a stressful thought onto a cloud and watch the wind slowly carry it away from you. If the clouds have quirky shapes, say aloud what they look like to you. Take five minutes and look up "types of clouds" online and see if you can decipher what their shapes are telling you about the weather. The sky is always there for you—it is constantly in the present. The next time you're getting in your head, find a way to look up and notice something in the sky to bring your awareness back to the moment.

NOVEMBER 29

Dreamland Meditation

Meditation can help you get to sleep when your mind won't turn off. Get comfortable in your bed by pulling the covers over your body and getting the pillows to support your neck and head. With your next few inhales, imagine the breath traveling down to the tips of your fingers and toes. Upon the exhale, sink farther into the mattress, noting the weight of your body upheld by the bed beneath you. Imagine that you see a few doors in front of you, and you turn the knob and walk through the one called "Dreamland." As you walk through, picture a tranquil scene with soothing colors and sounds, a place you can consider a retreat. In your dreamland, you are joyful and relaxed and safe. Use your imagination to decorate it in such a way that you'd want to come back on other nights.

NOVEMBER 30

See Love

Manifest the energy that's deep within you by remembering that you already have everything you need:

I see love everywhere.

DECEMBER 1

Identify Greatness

One way to ensure that you're not bogged down by your environment is to take moments throughout the day to notice what's pleasant or going well. If your negative thoughts are on a loop, gently acknowledge them, but turn your attention to saying aloud five things that happened that brought contentment or happiness. Did you have a delicious caffeinated drink? Did you talk to your best friend? Do you have a fun event coming up? Mindfulness practice is about the "return"—this means noticing when your mind has strayed to a negative headspace and bringing your awareness to another thought that brings you more positivity.

DECEMBER 2

Learn from Past Triggers

All humans experience suffering at the hands of others, even when they mean well. Set aside thirty minutes to dig deep and reflect. In your journal, answer the following: Who hurt your inner child? What patterns have you developed from your experiences of pain? How has that impacted your sensitivity to others?

DECEMBER 3

Accept Change

Change is not easy or always pleasant. Replace any statement where you're clinging to your former identity and transform it to:

I can be anyone I choose.

DECEMBER 4

Work a To-Do List

The next time you make a to-do list, grab some markers or colored pencils and cute it up. Draw little boxes you can check off and use color to highlight certain items that need more immediate attention. Feel free to add some tasks you did before getting a chance to make this to-do list, just so you can give yourself the validation of checking them off as "complete." Pick a small item on the list that you can accomplish as part of today's self-care practice. For example, say you've been meaning to go through and delete some old photos to free up storage in your phone. Check—complete!

DECEMBER 5

Color Meditation

Virtually any tangible or intangible thing is useful as an object of meditation. Using your visualization strengths, begin by looking around the space you're in and notice anything that jumps out as a color that isn't black or white. As you scan the room, note any objects that share the same color. Rest your gaze for at least ten seconds on each of your green plants and spend twenty seconds observing any objects that are a shade of blue. Shift your gaze with intention as if you were holding a camera steady, only focusing a lens when you are ready for the next shot. When your mind wanders, come back to the present moment by counting how many things in that room are in shades of red. Keep your attention on each object for the span of one full breath.

DECEMBER 6

I Am Responsible for My Own Energy

You oversee what energy comes in and comes out. Try not to convince yourself otherwise—your inner peace is yours. Say:

Nothing will disturb my peace unless I allow it to.

DECEMBER 7

What Comes Natural

Today is a day to touch on the past and to connect with your present. Set aside fifteen minutes to journal and reflect on the following questions: What did you learn about caring for others from your parents/caregivers? What aspects of your supportive and sensitive nature do you think you were born with?

DECEMBER 8

My Time Is Valuable

Caring for yourself means that you own this truth:

I will not make myself available for people who never prioritize me.

DECEMBER 9

Paint Watercolors

Do you know what self-care should feel like? Like lightly dipping a brush into a pastel watercolor paint and then into water, creating the most pleasant, calming swirl. Grab a watercolor set, a canvas, and create from memory a still life of veggies or fruits. Paint the way a rhythmic gymnast twirls a ribbon in the air, with each peaceful flourish sending away any unwelcome suffering. Focus your awareness on the colors you mix together, following the brush's strokes with a soft gaze.

DECEMBER 10

Stillness Meditation

On a particularly anxious day, your mind may feel like it won't let up after all your encounters and energy exchanges. No matter what you do, it seems as though the worrying and overthinking mind does not want to be restrained. Reassure yourself that at any point, you can easily come back to any stress that's on your mind—it will not disappear. Just for now, lie down and begin to sink into stillness. Just for now, breathe in steadily and breathe out, hearing how your exhale sounds like an ocean wave. Just for now, allow your mind to be free from any burdens. Imagine what it would feel like to have a clear mind and boundless, vibrant energy. Remind your wandering mind that just for now, you'll let go of anything that is not yours to carry.

DECEMBER 11

Let Old Habits Go

If you are still struggling to let go of old habits, here's a reminder:

Self-growth takes time. I am changing at a speed that is right for me.

DECEMBER 12

How Do I Respond to Change?

Although all humans struggle, empaths can feel particularly unsafe in the face of unpredictability or uncertainty. Reflect on how you typically respond to change. What is the most challenging part of change for you? What emotion does it cause? What could you do to make moments of change easier?

DECEMBER 13

I Am Evolving

You've been growing and changing. You deserve to celebrate that. Affirm:

I am evolving every day into a more peaceful being.

DECEMBER 14

Visit the Library

Going to the library is a pleasant experience, offering a quiet atmosphere, aisles full of books you could spend ages wandering, and a silent buzz of focus in the air. Have some fun by taking a random book off the shelf and try guessing what it will be about, just by looking at the cover. Pick out a book for your friend who hasn't been able to choose what to read next.

DECEMBER 15

Let Bygones Be Bygones

Think back to an experience, or conversation, that left you wondering if someone really "got" you. Did you feel like they were unable to understand you, or want to learn about who you are on a deeper level? How did that make you feel? Using the skills that you've developed so far, how else could you approach that moment to convey your individuality to this person?

DECEMBER 16

Navigate Crowds

Sometimes you might really want to leave a group gathering to recharge but you stay because you don't want to upset anyone by leaving. Be brave and listen to your inner voice. Say:

I am honoring my needs and that is a superpower.

DECEMBER 17

Touch a Tree

Grounding is beneficial for empaths when there is an overflow of emotions or stress present. As external forces have such a pull on empaths, grounding counters that and refocuses the spirit in the body. This leads to an increase in energy, improved sleep, faster wound healing, and more. For this grounding ritual, head out to your favorite tree or the closest one to you. Place the palm of your hand firmly on the tree trunk. Visualize the tree coaxing negative energy out of your body and replacing it with pure, positive energy from the earth's core, through its roots.

DECEMBER 18

Drumming Meditation

Sound is always a great focus for any meditation. Find an object that makes a beat when tapped or hit, such as a pot or pan, a desk, or even your lap. In this practice, you will use a drumming motion on your surface of choice to ground yourself in the present moment. Sit in a way that will make it comfortable for you to have the use of your arms and hands. Aligning with your breath, begin by tapping with alternating fingers, noticing the sensation of any vibrations. Continue the practice by increasing and decreasing the tempo, intensity, and cadence of your makeshift drum. Change up what you drum on to see how it creates a different sound. Note those differences as you become aware of them. When thoughts interrupt your attention, reorient your focus to where your hand meets the vibration of the surface.

DECEMBER 19

Heal with Crystals

It is believed that crystals emit positive, uplifting, and energizing vibrations that can help you achieve a calm mind and revitalized physical body. For this activity, use crystals to rejuvenate areas of your body that need extra attention. For instance, if your chest is sore, place on it your ideal crystal. Search online for a crystal energy reference guide to learn about which ones are right for you. Conversely, in lieu of purchasing crystals, search online to see if there's a nearby location that's a great spot to collect your own, like coasts, mines, or parks.

DECEMBER 20

Set Restful Intentions

The moment before you nod off to catch some z's is a great time to set an intention for your sleep. Say:

I can rest knowing that sleep will help restore energy back to my body, mind, and soul.

DECEMBER 21

Read a Magazine

Envision practicing self-care and help save a dying medium all in one fell swoop. Magazines are time capsules, giving you the pleasure of holding a book, but with articles and photo spreads that cover the topics relevant in the now. The content is a snapshot in time, making the reader feel as though they're uniquely in the know, kept abreast of monthly revelations in the architecture or celebrity or gardening world. There is a delightful energy to flipping through the pages, not knowing what story you'll stumble upon to next. Reading about anything else that's going on outside of your own personal world can be a momentary relief.

DECEMBER 22

Can I Stand in the Spotlight?

Imagine that someone close to you planned an entire day focused on you, spending time doing your favorite things and putting you in the spotlight. Set aside ten minutes to journal and reflect on how that might make you feel. Do you cringe or blush at the thought? Does it excite you?

DECEMBER 23

End the Day on a Positive Note

When you've taken so much time to make everyone else around you feel better, you've got to question why you wouldn't deserve the same sentiment. Say:

I give myself permission to feel good at the end of each day.

DECEMBER 24

Celebrate Accomplishments

Your willingness to help yourself by getting this book and prioritizing your wellness should be something to celebrate! In your journal, write a list of 10 achievements or successes from this past year that deserve praise. Was there a moment when you were able to set a clear boundary with someone who often sucked up your energy? Did you establish any mindfulness practices? Practice complimenting yourself or acknowledging the smallest of successes from the past year.

DECEMBER 25

Practicing Healthy Self-Talk

Reaffirm your mind's commitment to practicing healthy self-talk. Affirm:

I choose to replace negative self-talk with more uplifting speech.

DECEMBER 26

Sit with a Friend Meditation

There's no doubt you know at least a handful of other empaths who could use a bit of self-care themselves. You know their plight acutely, so invite them for a seated meditation with you for just five to ten minutes. As you both get settled in comfortable positions facing each other, start with your eyes closed. Your attention should rest lightly on observing your mind and body, noticing any sensations marking the energy in the room between you two. Allow any sounds of each other's breath or movement to rest at the entry of your ear canal. Observe any nuances that come up when sitting with someone else versus when you sit alone. As the energy flows between you, find safety and comfort in knowing you are connected to each other.

DECEMBER 27

My Superpower

Sure, being an empath comes with its hazards; however, it's important that you practice looking at it as an enormous strength by saying:

My empathic nature is a superpower.

DECEMBER 28

Find Joy in Earth and Nature

Empath vibes got you down? Tired of clichéd suggestions to drink more water and to go to the gym for self-care? This activity is a favorite among . . . anyone with a heart and eyes. Just stop whatever you're doing, pull up a clip of your favorite baby animal and let your heart swell. Check out The Dodo, a great website that features cute animals, animal duos, and rescue-rehabilitation stories that will melt you into a puddle without any emotional work on your part.

DECEMBER **29**

Self-Gratitude Meditation

You have completed a year of self-care practices that may not have felt feasible or accessible before you started this journey. It's time for a practice oriented around offering gratitude inward, because you deserve to acknowledge yourself for changing deeply engrained habits. Sit or lie down in your favorite meditating position—one where you are both comfortable and alert. Breathe in as much air as you can through your nose and impress yourself by breathing out for ten slow counts. Begin by thanking yourself for being present. Thank your mind for its ability to observe the world and to observe itself, all at the same time. Thank your intuition for guiding you to the right experiences. Thank your sensitivity for feeling people in need. Thank your body for always having the energy to hold you up and move you through life.

DECEMBER **30**

A Year of Reflection

Flip through all the writing you've done over the past year and then open your journal to a fresh page. Write about who you were before you decided to take self-care practice more seriously. Where are you today? What are you proud of? Will you continue filling up this journal or another notebook?

DECEMBER 31

Relishing *You*

You've made it through a whole freakin' book of self-care! The next steps of your growth will be because of the ones you took for the last year. Don't forget:

I honor my commitment to move forward in peace and contentment. I deserve to celebrate my progress.

Resources

Activity Ideas

The Box of Emotions: Designed by researchers at the Centre for the History of the Emotions in London, this set of cards is aimed at increasing emotion vocabulary necessary for appropriate emotion recognition used in mindfulness and meditation.

Emotional First Aid Kit: This set of cards from the School of Life gives you quick and thoughtful answers to tough situations so that you don't have to work as hard when providing support.

Mindful Self-Compassion Program: A course developed by Dr. Christopher Germer and Dr. Kristen Neff to be completed in either eight weeks or a five-day intensive that teaches you all the necessary skills to care for yourself—no matter what.

Apps

The following mobile apps are designed to teach you how to meditate and practice mindfulness throughout your entire day. There are many topics to choose from and you can even meditate virtually with people from across the globe.

Calm: Get it at Calm.com
Headspace: Get it at Headspace.com
Insight Timer: Get it at InsightTimer.com

Books

The following books are great resources to continue building your self-awareness and coping skills for the times when being an empath is a challenge.

Campion, Lisa. *Energy Healing for Empaths: How to Protect Yourself from Energy Vampires, Honor Your Boundaries, and Build Healthier Relationships.* Oakland, CA: New Harbinger Publications, 2021.

Carpenter, Krista. *The Empath's Workbook: Practical Strategies for Nurturing Your Unique Gifts and Living an Empowered Life.* Emeryville, CA: Rockridge Press, 2020.

Moorjani, Anita. *Sensitive Is the New Strong: The Power of Empaths in an Increasingly Harsh World.* London: Yellow Kite, 2021.

Orloff, Judith. *The Empath's Survival Guide: Life Strategies for Sensitive People.* Louisville, CO: Sounds True, 2017.

References

Germer, Christopher K. *The Mindful Path to Self-Compassion: Freeing Yourself from Destructive Thoughts and Emotions*. New York: Guilford Press, 2009.

Kabat-Zinn, Jon. *Full Catastrophe Living (Revised Edition): Using the Wisdom of Your Body and Mind to Face Stress, Pain, and Illness*. New York: Bantam Books, 2005.

Kabat-Zinn, Jon. *Wherever You Go, There You Are: Mindfulness Meditation in Everyday Life*. New York: Hachette Books, 2013.

Neff, Kristin. *Self-Compassion: The Proven Power of Being Kind to Yourself*. New York: HarperCollins, 2011.

Salzberg, Sharon. *Lovingkindness: The Revolutionary Art of Happiness*. Boston, MA: Shambhala Publications, 2002.

Index

Energy, 2, 6, 10, 36, 47, 56, 60,
    70, 76, 86, 87, 112, 141, 170
Experiences, 133, 139, 147

F

Fears, 71, 112
Feelings and emotions, 9, 12,
    13, 31, 46, 86, 108, 110, 134,
    149, 156, 165, 175, 179
Food and eating, 144, 151
Forgiveness, 45, 157
Freedom, 21
Frustration, 109

G

Giving back, 140
Goals, 149
Grace, 37
Gratitude, 25, 80, 117, 159, 182
Grounding, 19, 176
Growth, 35, 152, 174
Guilt, 15

H

Habits, 40, 173
Healing, 30, 53, 94, 128
Help, accepting, 58, 59, 163
Helplessness, 41
Hobbies, 113, 172
Holding space, 81
Household tasks, 82, 103, 169
Hypervigilance, 115

I

Identity, 1, 3, 105
Imagination, 68

Inner child, 18, 107
Inspiration, 44, 47
Intensity, 131
Intuition, 104, 105, 140
Isolation, 67

J

Joy, 63
Judgment, 135

K

Kindness, 148, 158

L

Laughter, 65, 101
Letting go, 90, 93, 144
Light, 80, 151
Limits, 78, 98
Listening, 34
Love, 167
Loving-kindness, 15

M

Manifestation, 27
Mantras, 85
Mental clarity, 87
Mental health, 48
Mental stimulation, 154
Mentors, 42
Movement, 117, 121, 141, 146
Museums, 153
Music, 50

N

Nature, 57, 59, 96, 127,
    135, 162, 166, 181
Needs, 29, 145, 152, 175

ACKNOWLEDGMENTS

Writing this book in the dead of winter, during a pandemic, in a short amount of time, would have felt impossible if not for some awesome humans. I'd like to thank Andrea, my editor, for her unwavering support and enthusiasm. A special note of gratitude goes out to the loveliest, empathic friends—Juliet and Katrina—who hyped me up, took care of Sunny, and reminded me of the self-care practices that I needed most. Dyl, thank you for being a charging station of sorts when I was almost out of battery.

ABOUT THE AUTHOR

 **Katie Krimer, MA, LCSW,** is a therapist at Union Square Practice, a thriving mental wellness practice in New York City. She is also the founder of Growspace, an authenticity and wellness coaching platform, where she supports humans along their self-growth journey. She authored *The Essential Self-Compassion Workbook for Teens* and *The Sh*t I Say to Myself.* Katie was born in Russia and immigrated to Brooklyn when she was five years old. She lives in New York and loves to hang out with her furry children, Sunny and Oats, and spends her free time on DIY projects around the house.